Culture, Contemplation, and Seminary formation

James Keating, Editor

The Institute for Priestly Formation
IPF Publications

CONTRIBUTORS

Fr. Earl K. Fernandes, S.T.D., is an official for the Apostolic Nunciature in Washington, D.C. and former dean of Mount St. Mary's Seminary in Cincinnati, Ohio.

Fr. Donald Haggerty, S.T.D., is a priest at St. Patrick's Cathedral in the Archdiocese of New York and former professor of Moral Theology at St. Joseph's Seminary in New York.

Keith Lemna, Ph.D., is Associate Professor of Systematic Theology at Saint Meinrad Seminary and School of Theology in St. Meinrad, Indiana.

Matthew Levering, Ph.D., is the James N. and Mary D. Perry, Jr. Chair of Theology at the University of St. Mary of the Lake, Mundelein Seminary, Illinois.

Mary McCaughey, D.D., is Professor of Theology at Oscott Seminary in Birmingham, England.

Christopher Ruddy, Ph.D., is Associate Professor of Historical and Systematic Theology at The Catholic University of America, Washington D.C.

Janet Smith, Ph.D., is the Father Michael McGivney Chair of Life Ethics at Sacred Heart Major Seminary in Detroit, Michigan.

NIHIL OBSTAT: Father Matthew J. Gutowski, JCL

IMPRIMATUR: Most Reverend George J. Lucas
                  Archbishop of Omaha, Nebraska
                  October 17, 2018

THE INSTITUTE FOR PRIESTLY FORMATION
IPF Publications
2500 California Plaza
Omaha, Nebraska 68178-0415
www.IPFPublications.com

Printed in the United States of America
ISBN-13: 978-0-9981164-5-7

Cover design by Timothy D. Boatright
Vistra Communications
Tampa, Florida

THE INSTITUTE FOR PRIESTLY FORMATION
Mission Statement

The Institute for Priestly Formation was founded to assist bishops in the spiritual formation of diocesan seminarians and priests in the Roman Catholic Church. The Institute responds to the need to foster spiritual formation as the integrating and governing principle of all aspects for priestly formation. Inspired by the biblical-evangelical spirituality of Ignatius Loyola, this spiritual formation has as its goal the cultivation of a deep interior communion with Christ; from such communion, the priest shares in Christ's own pastoral charity. In carrying out its mission, the Institute directly serves diocesan seminarians and priests as well as those who are responsible for diocesan priestly formation.

THE INSTITUTE FOR PRIESTLY FORMATION
Creighton University
2500 California Plaza
Omaha, Nebraska 68178-0415
www.priestlyformation.org
ipf@creighton.edu

TABLE OF CONTENTS

FOREWORD

As he was launching into his theological tour de force against Eunomius and his allies,[1] Gregory of Nazianzus begins by making it very clear that what we today call theology (a word that meant something quite different to him and his contemporaries) is, of necessity, an ascetical and contemplative discipline. This becomes a thread that is woven throughout his five *Orations*: before one approaches matters divine, one must begin with an *askesis*, a purification and a "honing," so that one might fruitfully contemplate the Mystery. Gregory was, by all accounts, one of the most learned figures in the fourth century, capable of subtle and nuanced theological distinctions. But he was also a practitioner of what von Balthasar, in the spirit of Gregory's contemporary Evagrius, once described as *die betende Theologie*: theology on one's knees. In this regard, Gregory was by no means a lone or singular voice, but the representative of a profound and living Tradition within Christianity, one which, while at times seemingly muted, has never lost its vigor or value. His "method" (no doubt an anachronistic term) was governed by a contemplative wonder in the presence of Truth, a Truth revealed partially and gradually in the history of the people of Israel, and finally and definitively in the Incarnate Word, the man Jesus Christ.

The essays contained in this volume offer reflections on the contemplative nature of the theological discipline, with a view to assisting those who have been entrusted with formation of men for the priesthood. These essays are an invitation to think more deeply and, perhaps, even to reconceive the way in which we think about intellectual formation and its relation to the other dimensions of priestly formation. The term "contemplative" might itself suggest that the content of this volume is principally about the spiritual life. In fact, the term contemplation expresses—perhaps better than any other—the integration of the intellectual and the spiritual life, the dynamic between faith and reason, between prayer and study, between the experience of the believer and the objective fact of the Mystery, in the encounter which is the act of faith.

The life of the mind is no threat to the life of the spirit. To consider the intellectual life a threat to the life of prayer reveals a grave misunderstanding of one or both of these terms. We do an enormous service to the men in our care, and to the Church we all serve, by inculcating in seminarians the harmony, and even coincidence, of what Jean Leclercq described as "the love of learning and the desire for God."

Monsignor Michael Heintz, Ph.D.
Academic Dean, Mount St. Mary's Seminary
Emmitsburg, Maryland

NOTES

1. *Oration* 27 (of *Orations* 27-31, which came to be known as the "Theological Orations"), delivered probably late summer 380, in Constantinople; for a fine edition, see *On God and Christ: The Five Theological Orations and Two Letters to Cledonius*, trans. F. Williams and L. Wickham (Crestwood, NY: St Vladimir's Seminary Press, 2002); for context and a shrewd appraisal, see J. McGuckin, *Saint Gregory of Nazianzus: An Intellectual Biography* (Crestwood, NY: St Vladimir's Seminary Press, 2001), 277-310.

CONTEMPLATING JESUS RISEN

MATTHEW LEVERING

What does seminary formation have to do with contemplation? According to Father Joseph Ratzinger in 1973, a priest must learn, as a seminarian, "not to preach himself, but rather the faith of the Church"—and even for the Apostles, the faith of the Church was "a message that infinitely exceeded them."[1] Father Ratzinger continues: "What is at issue is that the Word of God remain in this world. . . . The priest is here so that the Word of God remains."[2] What, then, is the fundamental "message," without which the "Word of God" will not remain in this world?

In seeking to articulate the fundamental content of the Gospel, biblical scholars often turn to the Apostle Paul's creedal summary in 1 Corinthians 15:1-8. Clearly, this creedal summary does not contain everything, but it stands as a good starting point. Paul begins with a stirring preface: "Now I am reminding you, brothers, of the gospel I preached to you, which you indeed received and in which you also stand. Through it you are also being saved, if you hold fast to the word I preached to you" (1 Cor 15:1-2). He then articulates the basic elements of this saving Gospel: "For I handed on to you as of first importance what I also received: that Christ died for our sins in accordance with the scriptures; that he was buried; that he was raised on the third day in accordance with the scriptures; that he appeared to Cephas, then to the Twelve" (1 Cor 15:3-5). Paul continues by listing appearances of the risen Jesus to "more than five hundred brothers at once" (1 Cor 15:6), to James, and to himself. It will be clear, then, that the Gospel by which we are saved involves, preeminently, Christ's Cross and Resurrection.

Likewise, according to the Book of Acts, when the Apostles were sent forth to proclaim the Gospel to Israel and to the whole world, they focused on the fact that Jesus had risen from the dead. Had He not risen, they could not have proclaimed Him to be the Messiah of Israel, and they could not have received the outpouring of the Spirit in His inaugurated kingdom. But, in fact, as Peter proclaims at Pentecost, "God raised this Jesus; of this we are all witnesses. Exalted at the right hand of God, he received the promise of the holy Spirit from the Father and poured it forth, as you (both) see and hear" (Acts 2:32-33). When Paul preaches in Antioch, he makes the heart of his preaching the fact that "God raised him from the dead, and for many days he appeared to those who had come up with him from Galilee to Jerusalem. These are [now] his witnesses before the people" (Acts 13:30-31). Similarly, at the Areopagus in Athens, preaching to the most erudite philosophers of his day, Paul builds his sermon to the following climax: God "has established a day on which he will 'judge the world with justice' through a man he has appointed, and he has provided confirmation for all by raising him from the dead" (Acts 17:31).

When Paul later proclaims this Gospel to King Agrippa and to Porcius Festus, the Roman governor, Paul again concludes on the note that Jesus Christ has risen from the dead. But in response, "Festus said in a loud voice, You are mad, Paul; much learning is driving you mad'" (Acts 26:24). It seemed to Festus that the proclamation of Jesus' Resurrection was crazy. Likewise, among the philosophers and educated elite at the Areopagus in Athens, "When they heard about resurrection of the dead, some began to scoff" (Acts 17:32).

What does this preaching mean for the seminarian of today? According to St. John Paul II's Apostolic Exhortation *Pastores Dabo Vobis*, the priest must be "[d]eeply rooted in the truth and charity of Christ" and "impelled by the desire and imperative to proclaim Christ's salvation to all."[3] In contemporary culture, however, bookstores are full of popular books about Jesus that deny the truth of His Resurrection. Reza Aslan's bestselling *Zealot: The Life and Times of Jesus of Nazareth* exemplifies the trend.[4] Aslan argues that if one wishes to claim that Jesus rose to glorified life after three days, then one has to face the fact that such a claim "defies all logic, reason, and sense," and, furthermore, that such a claim cannot be counted as "historical."[5] If priests are to be able effectively "to proclaim Christ's salvation to all," then priests will need to have answers to the onslaught of publications aimed at destroying faith in Jesus' Resurrection, which stands at the very heart of the Gospel.

At the same time, *Pastores Dabo Vobis* also rightly insists that priests require "an interior life, a life of intimacy with God, a life of prayer and contemplation."[6] Contemplation has many aspects, and the term can mean the height of personal prayer, in which Christians behold the triune God in a

non-discursive, mystical darkness caused by the interior presence of the Divine Light.[7] The term can also mean simply "a
deeper interior life," in which the Christian at prayer experiences what Father Donald Haggerty calls "the provocation of
God's hidden presence to the soul."[8] Lastly, and most relevant
to my purposes, the term can mean the contemplation of the
truth of Jesus through meditative reflection upon the scriptural word.

In this essay, I hope to show that Jesus' "humanity is
appropriate to his divinity" (in the words of David Bentley
Hart[9]): in the mysteries of His humanity, above all in His
Crucifixion and Resurrection, Jesus reveals to us the radical
inbreaking of Divine truth, best known through the act of
contemplation. My essay has three steps. First, I attend to
certain elements of what Thomas Aquinas has to say about
contemplation. Although Aquinas generally has in view the
height of contemplative union with the triune God, I focus
upon contemplation of Christ and upon the contemplative
fruits that arise from the study of Christ. Second, I examine
Pope Benedict XVI's effort to perceive the face of Christ
through the biblical portraits of Christ. In his *Jesus of Nazareth: Part Two*, his contemplative meditation upon the New
Testament narratives about Jesus' Resurrection provides him
with grounds for judging the historicity of Jesus' Resurrection. Third, I survey the case for the credibility of Christian
claims that is offered by Hans Urs von Balthasar in his short
book *Love Alone Is Credible*, originally published in German
in 1963.[10] Von Balthasar argues that the truth of Christian
claims does not ultimately depend upon the structure of history or the dynamism of the human heart, or even upon historical data that can be advanced in favor of the credibility of

what the Bible records. Rather, the truth of Christian claims
will only be perceived when one contemplates the radical
Divine love that is revealed in Christ.[11] By bringing together
these insights of Aquinas, Ratzinger, and von Balthasar, I
hope to show that the formation of seminarians to know
the truth of Jesus' Resurrection requires that seminarians be
formed in the path of contemplation. If seminarians are not
contemplatives, their witness to the truth of Jesus' Resurrection is imperiled.

Thomas Aquinas on Christian Contemplation

In his *Summa Theologica*, Thomas Aquinas comments that
"the end [or goal] of the contemplative life is the consideration of truth."[12] He argues that we are prepared for the
contemplative life by the moral virtues, which cause "peace
and cleanness of heart."[13] But the contemplative life in itself
is "an act of reason."[14] Describing what this act of reason
involves, Aquinas notes that the completion of contemplation, its "last and crowning act," is found in "the contemplation itself of the truth."[15] To get to this point, however, can
be difficult, not only for fallen natural reason but also for
reason enlightened supernaturally by faith.

I focus here on contemplation of truth known in faith.
The steps that pertain to contemplation of revealed truth
include hearing the words of teachers, praying for God's
instruction, reading Scripture, and personal study or meditation.[16] Agreeing with Gregory the Great, Aquinas holds
that the truth that stands at the center of all contemplation
is Divine truth: contemplation properly seeks to rest in the
knowledge of God. Such contemplation is the goal of all
human life, since the beatitude of the blessed will consist

primarily in eternal contemplative union with God, whom we shall "see . . . face to face [cf. 1 Cor 13:12]."[17]

Even now, however, we receive "a certain inchoate beatitude" insofar as we are able to contemplate God "indistinctly, in a mirror" (1 Cor 13:12).[18] Indebted to Richard of St. Victor, Aquinas affirms that there are six "steps whereby we ascend by means of creatures to the contemplation of God."[19] These steps include receiving sense impressions; forming concepts about sensible things; making judgments of truth about sensible things; considering these judgments of truth in themselves; considering intelligible things (such as the soul, angels, and God in His unity) "that are unattainable by means of sensibles, but which the reason is able to grasp"; and considering divinely revealed intelligible things (God in his Trinity) that "reason can neither discover or grasp."[20] These steps indicate not only the path of contemplation, but also the limitations of contemplation in this life. In the present life, the grace of rapture—such as Aquinas believes Paul experienced[21]—is necessary for humans to contemplate the Divine essence itself.[22] Otherwise, in the present life, we always need conceptual judgments of truth as the basis of our contemplation of Divine truth. We do not contemplate our own concepts, but rather, we contemplate "*in them* the purity of the intelligible truth."[23]

What motivates the contemplation of God in this life and in eternal life? Aquinas answers that love fuels contemplation.[24] The act of contemplation causes spiritual delight, indeed spiritual delight of such force as to surpass all other human delights (just as charity greatly surpasses all merely human loves).[25] This delight in contemplation produces, in turn, yet greater charity. Thus, charity is not only at the root but also at the end of contemplation. Aquinas states that the completion of charity, its "ultimate perfection," is "that the divine truth be not only seen but also loved."[26] With respect to the delight of contemplation, Aquinas cites two Psalms, the latter of which applies only to the beatific vision: "O taste and see that the Lord is good!" (Ps 34:8) and "thou givest them drink from the river of thy delights" (Ps 36:8).[27]

Aquinas holds that Mary of Bethany, sister of Martha, exemplifies the contemplative life.[28] In the Gospel of Luke, Jesus praises Mary of Bethany for choosing the one necessary thing, "the better part" (Lk 10:42). That "better part" consists in sitting "beside the Lord at his feet" and listening to His words (Lk 10:39). Mary is the model of the contemplative because, by hearing the words of Christ, she contemplates Christ—and, thereby, contemplates Divine truth. In the first chapter of the *Summa Contra Gentiles*, Aquinas notes that truth is "the ultimate end of the whole universe," since God is infinite intelligence.[29] We know this truth, says Aquinas, above all through Jesus Christ. In the Gospel of John, "divine Wisdom testifies that He has assumed flesh and come into the world in order to make the truth known: 'For this was I born, and for this came I into the world, that I should give testimony to the truth' (John 18:37)."[30] Indeed, since Christ is the Incarnate Word of God, Aquinas emphasizes that "divine truth" has personally revealed Himself in Christ: "divine truth . . . is truth in person."[31]

To know such divine truth in Christ, and to love this divine truth and be configured to it intellectually and morally, is to be joined "to God in friendship."[32] Aquinas has in view John 15:15, where Jesus tells His disciples, "I have called you friends, for all that I have heard from my Father I have made known to you."[33] In Christ, God has willed to communicate His own beatitude to us and has, therefore, established a true friendship or fellowship in divine goods with us.[34] Agreeing with Pope Innocent III, Aquinas holds that "Christ's action is our instruction."[35] The Incarnation instructs us about God's infinite goodness because "it belongs to the essence of goodness to communicate itself to others."[36] Because Christ is the Incarnate Son of God, each of His actions and words instructs us in some way about who God is. Contemplating God's truth, then, requires, above all, the consideration of Jesus Christ in His words and deeds. When we contemplate Christ, we are never contemplating a mere man.[37]

What does Aquinas think we learn by contemplating Christ in His Crucifixion? We learn a great deal about Christ's sacred humanity and about how we are called to act because Christ on the Cross "set us an example of obedience, humility, constancy, justice, and the other virtues . . . which are requisite for man's salvation."[38] Do we learn anything about God? Aquinas considers that we learn the greatness of God's love for us in a manner that makes clear how intensely personal God's love for us is.[39] What, then, do we learn about God by contemplating Christ's Resurrection? Aquinas states that first of all, we learn the truth of the Divine justice, "to which it belongs to exalt them who humble themselves for God's sake, according to Luke 1:52: *He hath put down the mighty from their seat, and hath exalted the humble.*"[40] Christ's love and obedience, as the Incarnate Son, are answered by the triune God's justice in resurrecting Christ. The Paschal Mystery of Christ reveals God's goodness, mercy, love, and justice. To contemplate Jesus risen is to contemplate these divine truths.

Indeed, in Christ's actions, and in Christ's communion with His Father and His breathing forth of the Spirit upon His Disciples, the entire Holy Trinity reveals Himself to the contemplative. Commenting on John 14:9, where Jesus tells the disciple Philip that "he who has seen me has seen the Father," Aquinas notes that Jesus "is saying in effect: If you knew me, you would know the Father . . . because you would have already seen him by seeing me."[41] As Jesus' friends, we see the risen Jesus in His "truth in person," His truth that is His love that manifests the Father. Furthermore, Jesus remains fully present to the contemplative eye, though now in His sacramental mode in the Eucharist.[42]

In sum, contemplation of divine truth finds a rich path in the contemplation of "truth in person," Jesus Christ. Contemplating the risen Christ reveals the wondrous justice of God in exalting Christ; and since the Resurrection is never cut off from the Cross (or from the defeat of sin and death), contemplating the risen Christ also reveals the love of God for sinners. Does such contemplation, however, help us in knowing that Christ's Resurrection really happened? It may seem that since contemplation of the risen Christ is grounded in faith, it cannot assist us in assessing the historical credibility of Christ's Resurrection. To investigate this question of whether a faith-filled contemplation of Christ can help us to defend the historicity of Christ's Resurrection, I turn to the work of Joseph Ratzinger/Pope Emeritus Benedict XVI.

Joseph Ratzinger on Seeing the Face of Jesus

In the Foreword to the first volume of his *Jesus of Nazareth*, Ratzinger notes that due to the findings of much historical-critical research over the past two centuries, the figure of Jesus has become more difficult to contemplate. The Jesus of the Gospels can seem not only an ambiguous figure, but also a figure whom the evangelists largely invented, behind which stands a real but largely inaccessible "historical Jesus."[43] Ratzinger recognizes that faith in Jesus is unlikely to endure if one grants that "the *man* Jesus was so completely different from the picture that the Evangelists painted of him and that the Church, on the evidence of the Gospels, takes as the basis of her preaching."[44]

In response, Ratzinger argues for trusting the Gospels. First, he observes that the historical-critical reconstructions tend to contradict each other, which suggests that the New Testament's witness may be more plausible than any reconstruction. Second, he proposes that historical-critical exegesis must be complemented by canonical exegesis, which, through its focus on Scripture as a unity, helps one to "see that the Old and New Testaments belong together" and to recognize (here moving to the level of faith) that Jesus is "the key to the whole," without denying the historical diversity of the texts.[45] Once Scripture is recognized for what it is—a coherent whole—it becomes possible to appreciate how each particular text contributes to a greater work being accomplished by God Himself. One is, thereby, strengthened in one's trust in the Gospels as part of a divinely authored whole, whose full meaning is unlocked by Christ's life, Death, and Resurrection.

Third, Ratzinger makes a positive case for the coherence of the New Testament's portraits of Jesus. He states, "Though the New Testament writings display a many-layered struggle to come to grips with the figure of Jesus, they exhibit a deep harmony despite all their differences."[46] Their harmony consists in their revelation of "a way and a figure that are worthy of belief," by contrast to the unimpressive figure portrayed by modern reconstructions.[47] The main lines of the New Testament's testimony to Jesus reveal a person whose words and deeds provide both a worthy fulfillment to God's promises to Israel and a worthy revelation of the God of Israel. This worthiness cannot be chalked up to mere successful inventiveness. As Ratzinger says, "Unless there had been something extraordinary in what happened, unless the person and the words of Jesus radically surpassed the hopes and expectations of the time, there is no way to explain why he was crucified or why he made such an impact"—including, within two decades after His death, being hailed as equal to God and owed all worship.[48] Ratzinger suggests that only the Jesus of the New Testament writings can account for both the coherence of the biblical texts, viewed as a whole, and the actual impact of Jesus Himself. No other version of "Jesus" can do so. It follows that we have good reason to "trust the Gospels," even as we continue to benefit from historical-critical research.[49]

By means of these arguments, Ratzinger seeks to reinvigorate contemporary contemplation of Jesus. We can only contemplate Him if the Gospels present us with the essential truth about Him. In the three volumes of his *Jesus of Nazareth*, Ratzinger's goal is to continue his own contemplative "search 'for the face of the Lord' (cf. Ps 27:8)."[50] Ratzinger explains that his project is not an attempt to compose a life of Jesus, since "[e]xcellent [historical-critical] studies are already available concerning chronological and topographical questions to do with the life of Jesus."[51] Nor is Ratzinger's project an attempt to write a Christology, whether "from above" or "from below." Instead, the intention of his project

follows lines closer to "the theological treatise on the mysteries of the life of Jesus, presented in its classic form by Saint
Thomas Aquinas."[52] He comments, however, that his project
differs from that of Aquinas since he is consciously aiming to
show that the New Testament's Jesus is the real Jesus, a point
that Aquinas takes for granted. Ratzinger strives to combine
historical-critical, canonical, and patristic exegetical modes
in a manner that deliberately fosters a "personal encounter"
with the Jesus who fulfilled Israel's Scriptures and made such
a huge impact.[53] It is in and through this personal encounter,
made possible by contemplation, that we can come to know
with certitude the truth about Jesus.

Given his combination of contemplative and historical
goals, what happens when Ratzinger turns his attention to
Jesus' Resurrection? Can Ratzinger's approach to defending
the truth of Jesus' Resurrection be that of a contemplative who is able to "taste and see that the Lord is good"
(Ps 34:9)? In his discussion of Jesus' Resurrection in *Jesus
of Nazareth: Part Two*, Ratzinger first remarks that the New
Testament (and Christianity) would not work without the
Resurrection of Jesus. Had Jesus remained dead, Jesus could
not have inaugurated the kingdom or fulfilled any promises
of the Old Testament.[54] The New Testament's claims about
Jesus (for example, that He is the Messiah) would fall to the
ground if He had not been raised, since there would be no
plausible basis for believing Jesus' claims about Himself.
Ratzinger concludes that the first Christians must at least have
strongly *believed* Jesus to have been raised from the dead. He
also makes much of the fact that the Resurrection of Jesus
offers a fulfillment that the Old Testament itself could not
anticipate, since in Second-Temple Jewish eschatology "a

resurrection into definitive otherness in the midst of the continuing old world was not foreseen."[55] The unexpected newness of the Resurrection of Jesus is linked to the unexpected newness of the Crucifixion of the Messiah. Neither event could have been anticipated.

Ratzinger divides the Resurrection testimony in the New Testament into two kinds: "confessional" and "narrative." When, as in numerous letters of Paul, the proclamation of Jesus' Resurrection is found in a confession of faith and linked with reception of salvation, the character of Jesus' *Death* becomes especially important for understanding the truth of His Resurrection. Specifically, His Death is one that reveals God's humility and love. Rooted in God's love, Jesus' Death fits with the Divine love shown in Jesus' Resurrection. With respect to the earliest confessions of faith, Jesus' Death also requires that His tomb be empty. No testimony to Jesus' Resurrection could have been possible in the Jerusalem of Jesus' day had His corpse still been present in the tomb. Thus, we cannot separate contemplation of God's love in Jesus crucified and risen, from historical arguments for the truth of Jesus' Resurrection.

Ratzinger notes that the "confessional" testimonies to Jesus' Resurrection condense the elements that appear in more detail in the "narrative" testimonies. The narratives testify that Jesus appeared in His risen flesh in Jerusalem and in Galilee. Just as the women remained at the Cross, so they were the first to discover that He had been raised. Paul, after Jesus' Ascension, heard Jesus' voice and perceived Him as a blinding light; but, so far as we know, Paul did not see or touch Jesus' risen flesh. By contrast, in the Gospels, although the risen Jesus often goes unrecognized and is able to enter through closed doors and appear or disappear suddenly, the ongoing physicality of His risen body receives emphasis, since He eats and allows Himself to be touched. Ratzinger suggests that the Old Testament theophanies, in particular the appearance of an angel who represents God, prefigure the Resurrection appearances of Jesus through their combination of human form and transcendence of the "laws of material existence," although they lack the new and decisive claim that a specific person's corpse has been gloriously raised.[56] Ratzinger also connects the risen Jesus' sharing meals with His disciples with the way in which covenants in the Old Testament were sealed and sacrifices were offered. What the disciples discovered in the appearances of the risen Jesus, Ratzinger concludes, was that "the Lord is drawing the disciples into a new covenant-fellowship with him and with the living God," a new "table fellowship."[57]

Ratzinger also comments upon the combination of the glorious transformation of Jesus' body and His manifestation of this radical newness to His disciples *within* history. This combination accords with the disciples' testimony that His Cross and Resurrection inaugurate the eschatological kingdom without thereby *ending* history. In addition, as Ratzinger remarks, the evangelizing zeal of Jesus' disciples, their willingness to give up their lives for the truth of their testimony despite the fact that regular history was still ongoing, makes sense only in light of Jesus' actual Resurrection. After His Crucifixion by the Romans, His followers would not have identified him as the Messiah and given their lives for Him without "a real encounter, coming to them from outside, with . . . the self-revelation and verbal communication of the risen Christ."[58] Lastly, Ratzinger defends the fittingness of the risen Jesus revealing Himself to only a few persons. Just as God chose Israel as a small people in order to make Himself known to the whole world, God in the risen Christ makes Himself known to a relatively few eyewitnesses in order to spread the good news—not of Divine power and domination but of intimately personal Divine love as the source of true communion among people.

Ratzinger's key point, for my purposes here, is simply this: there could never have been a contemplation of Jesus— a contemplation that saw in Him the fulfillment of the Scriptures—had Jesus not actually showed Himself to His disciples as risen from the dead. The very fact that we are today able to contemplate Jesus is testimony to the historicity of His Resurrection. Put otherwise, the New Testament could not have been written without the disciples' belief in Jesus' Resurrection. This belief required strong evidence in order to be upheld. Thus, the *very existence* of the New Testament's surprising but coherent fulfillment of the Old.Testament not only enables us to contemplate the real Jesus, but also ties our contemplation to the actual historicity of Jesus' Resurrection.

Hans Urs von Balthasar: The Apologetics of Love

Through Ratzinger's work, we have seen that our ability to contemplate the face of Jesus is rooted in Scriptures whose existence and coherence arguably depends upon the historicity of Jesus' Resurrection. Contemplation of Jesus, then, immediately draws us toward evidence for the truth of His Resurrection. But now, we can make an additional step, guided by Aquinas's insight that Jesus is "truth in person."[59] If the face of Jesus were not the face of love, then contemplation of Jesus as risen would be impossible because it would be implausible. Only the image of Divine love could be worthy of contemplation and worthy of unique Resurrection in the midst of history. In contemplation, we perceive the truth of Jesus' Resurrection in light of Jesus' whole life and of God's revelation in Israel's Scriptures. We know the truth of Jesus' Resurrection, in part, due to the conformity of His Resurrection with the love that He embodies and reveals; and our contemplation is fueled by this love.

In *Love Alone Is Credible*, Hans Urs von Balthasar refers to Augustine's view that the entire Scripture is about "the reign of charity," and von Balthasar also cites Blaise Pascal to the effect that Scripture's object is love.[60] Von Balthasar's theme in this short book is what makes Christianity credible. He argues that for the Church Fathers, Christianity was credible because it fulfilled the Old Testament and fulfilled world history by converting the pagan idolaters. Christianity was the true wisdom, the true *Logos* of the cosmos. In the Enlightenment, however, the specifically Christian elements began to be discarded. Christianity became simply the bearer of philosophical truths to the whole world, thereby demonstrating the inadequacy of this path of verification of the truth of Christianity.

In the modern period, then, "the locus of verification" of Christianity shifted "from the increasingly demythologized cosmos . . . to the human being, who recapitulated the entire world in himself."[61] Rather than defending the truth of Christianity by contemplating the *Logos* of the cosmos, now defenders of Christianity began to contemplate the human being. For instance, Pascal argues for the truthfulness of Christianity on the grounds of Christianity's profound witness to the human being's simultaneous greatness and wretchedness. But in Baruch Spinoza, Immanuel Kant, and others, the truth of Judaism and Christianity is determined by the degree to which belief conforms with universal ethical norms established by human reason. These philosophers search in Christianity for a rational religion that accords with the measure of human rationality. On this view, Jesus Christ is credible to the degree that He exemplifies rational religion and rational ethics.

Ludwig Feuerbach turns this idea into an awe for the self-transcending capacity of the human mind, and Friedrich Schleiermacher turns it into a consciousness of our absolute dependence, which comprises the "redemption" that Christ offers. Later thinkers present Christ as the ultimate expression of absolute spirit's self-manifestation or of existential detachment from anxiety. Others present Christianity as the fulfillment of religious subjectivity in the will's ascent toward "absolute decision" (Maurice Blondel) or the intellect's dynamism toward the infinite (Pierre Rousselot).[62] Still others, including Max Scheler and Martin Buber, point to the I-Thou structure of human rationality, the face-to-face encounter that unveils the "divine" depths of human existence and that Jesus supremely enacts. Von Balthasar credits two modern philosophers with resisting this reduction of revelation to the unfolding of the deepest dynamism of human subjectivity: Johann Georg Hamann, who insists that God's self-revelation as self-humbling love is so radical that it cannot be anticipated, and Søren Kierkegaard, who argues that Christ can be known only as absolute paradox (a point followed by Léon Bloy and Fyodor Dostoevsky).

Von Balthasar argues that that "Christianity disappears the moment it allows itself to be dissolved into a transcendental precondition of human self-understanding in thinking or living, knowledge or deed."[63] It may, therefore, seem that the only possible evidence for the truth of Christian claims is an "extrinsicist" one that relies upon proofs from *history*. But von Balthasar proposes a third way, between immanentism (proofs from subjectivity) and extrinsicism (proofs from history). This third way involves the entrance of a Thou who remains completely unexpected, an encounter that cannot be anticipated in any way but that possesses "compelling plausibility."[64] The Logos appears as absolutely free and unexpected Love, radiant with Divine beauty or glory. We cannot reduce this Logos to the level of human love; but rather, we can only "adore it from a reverent distance whenever we perceive it," since its beauty overwhelms us even while bestowing upon us the gift of "an inconceivable intimacy" with the God who (as Love) is radically Other from us.[65] Since human love is marked by self-interest and by the prospect of death, difference itself inevitably becomes an enemy of love. By contrast, the Love revealed in Christ, through His embrace of radical difference in his radical self-humbling, can only be shocking and scandalous, revealing our "creaturely love" to be, by comparison, "nonlove."[66]

Von Balthasar makes clear that Divine Love, as grace, stirs up and awakens love within us. He insists upon a prior "unilateral" movement of Divine Love toward us, a movement that in itself brings about our response, as in Mary's *fiat*. Nothing in Scripture can be adequately understood when faith is bracketed, since the Logos (Love) enables the witnesses to know Him in faith. Von Balthasar states, "A 'critical' study of this Word as a human, historical document will therefore necessarily run up against the reciprocal, nuptial relationship of word and faith in the witness of the Scripture."[67] Faith suffuses the biblical testimony to Jesus' Resurrection; and, therefore, the testimony, when read by non-believers looking solely for evidence, will be only partially understood, at best. Von Balthasar argues that "the site from which love can be observed and generated cannot itself lie outside of love (in the 'pure logicity' of so-called science); it can lie only there, where the matter itself lies—namely, in the drama of love."[68]

To deem the narratives about Jesus' Resurrection to be historically credible, then, cannot be separated from entering by grace into the "drama of love" and contemplating the whole revelation of Divine Love. Von Balthasar encourages those who seek to know the truth of Jesus to possess "a receptive disposition of pure letting-be," of emptying or surrendering oneself in welcoming the Divine Love that manifests itself unmistakably in Jesus.[69] Indeed, the Divine Word (Love) generates this receptive word (of love) on the part of the believer. If Jesus' Cross were merely an *unintended* Death, then His teaching, from the beginning of His public ministry through His Last Supper, would lose its sense. The Logos or logic of His teaching and of His Cross is that self-sacrifice in Love (complete powerlessness) is the nature of Divine power, by contrast to the empty power of those who rely on anything other than self-sacrificial love. Such a Word, grounded in such a deed, might seem to be that of a fanatic, but His words show "no fanatical Dionysian exaltation" but only perfect obedience to a Divine mission of Love.[70] In his utter kenosis or self-emptying, Divine majesty shows itself as Love going to shocking lengths, fully bearing what is opposed to God.

Von Balthasar lays stress not so much upon the Resurrection of Jesus but upon His Ascension, which enables us to participate in a love that does not cling to the other but lets the other go, as befits the self-surrendering Divine Love. This experience is never separated from the Cross because we now participate liturgically in Christ's Cross in a manner that makes present in our very midst "the living and resurrected Christ" in the Eucharist, as an eschatological sign of the new creation.[71] At the same time, von Balthasar pays extensive attention to the judgment of this world, a judgment caused by human resistance to Love—and a judgment that, von Balthasar argues, Christ bears to the fullest extent, thereby fulfilling all God's covenantal promises and exposing "the fiery abyss of divine love."[72]

Von Balthasar holds that only when such self-surrendering Love is recognized does Christianity (including Jesus' Resurrection) become credible; and when such Love is recognized, we realize that only such Love could be God. As von Balthasar puts it, "Love alone is credible; nothing else can be believed, and nothing else ought to be believed."[73] This God alone, in His "inconceivable and senseless act of love," is that which nothing greater can be thought.[74] We could not have raised our minds to this God, whether through cosmic or anthropological structures, had not this God revealed Himself as shocking Love. On this basis, von Balthasar holds that the "contemplative life" names the life of complete self-surrender in love to Love, whether this takes shape through active works in the world or solely through study and prayer.[75] He warns against reducing the contemplative life to one of knowledge, since in fact, the contemplation of Love primarily involves self-surrendering love, not any other form of ascent.

At the same time, human action never has priority, since only the contemplation of Love can have priority. Von Balthasar observes, "Whoever does not come to know the face of God in contemplation will not recognize it in action, even when it reveals itself to him in the face of the oppressed and humiliated."[76] In this sense, prayer and the Eucharist—which is a contemplative remembrance, a "contemplation in love and the communion of love with love"—have absolute priority.[77]

In the lives of the saints, von Balthasar finds this utter grounding in self-surrendering Love. He states, "The sole credibility of the Church Christ founded lies, as he [Jesus] himself says, in the saints, as those who sought to set all things on the love of Christ alone."[78] In light of the self-surrendering love of the saints, Jesus' Resurrection has all the credibility that it needs. Von Balthasar observes that the Incarnation is a uniting of God and human existence, for the purpose of the Son's radical liquidation or self-sacrifice on the Cross. The Resurrection of Jesus, then, is the Son's reception—and gift to the Father—of His "sacrificed nature (and thus the world) transformed and eternalized."[79] The Resurrection of Jesus is the *eternalizing* of Jesus' radical self-surrender, His mode of living human existence. The risen Christ hands the whole world, now in its eternalized form of self-surrendering love, to the Father.

From von Balthasar's perspective, then, the search for historical grounds on which to measure or defend the credibility of the Resurrection of Jesus is myopic or, to use von Balthasar's phrase for historical apologetics, "extrinsicist." The real grounds for the historical credibility of Jesus' Resurrection can be seen only when we perceive and contemplate the full picture—namely, the manifestation of self-surrendering Love, bringing the whole world to the Father in an eternalized gift of self-surrender, as exhibited by the saints. The historicity of the Resurrection of Jesus cannot be separated from the entirety of Love's manifestation in Christ; and the historical truth of Jesus' Resurrection will be known only by the person who *in (graced) love* can see the inbreaking of shocking Divine Love in Christ and, in witness to Him, in His saints. Contemplation of Jesus' Resurrection, therefore, bears within it a knowledge of the historical truth of Jesus' Resurrection, when contemplation is truly contemplation in and of love.

Conclusion

Each of these three perspectives has distinctive strengths. The essay began with Aquinas, who emphasizes that while the object of contemplation is truth, the motivation of contemplation is love. The truth contemplated by Christians is not merely abstract truth, but "truth in person," truth revealed in Christ. All Christ's actions instruct us; we contemplate the Divine Father by contemplating Christ's human words and deeds. If Christ's words and deeds were unworthy of the Father or did not manifest the love and justice and mercy of the God of Israel, then they could not be true.

Aquinas's contemplation of Christ, however, does not ask historical questions about the credibility of the Gospel portraits of Christ. Ratzinger brings such historical questions to the forefront. He recognizes that Christian contemplation and faith are impeded today by doubts about whether the biblical portraits of Jesus are trustworthy. If we cannot trust the biblical portraits of Jesus, how can we contemplate Him? Thus, contemplation and historical questioning now have to go together. Ratzinger holds that contemplation of Jesus reveals the wholeness and coherence of the Bible itself, with Jesus as the key to this coherence. When we contemplate Jesus, we see that the New Testament's testimony about His Resurrection could not easily have been invented and that only the Gospels' presentations of Jesus enable us to understand the actual impact that He had. We find that had the Disciples not firmly believed that Jesus had been raised, they could not have written what they did about Jesus; and the canonical coherence of what they wrote itself bears witness to the truth of Jesus' Resurrection. In Jesus' Cross and Resurrection, we contemplate the scope of God's redeeming love, and we see fulfilled the intimacy with God for which Israel yearned. Contemplating Jesus risen, we observe that His risen body bears eschatological glory within history—as befits an inaugurated kingdom that does not end the course of history. We also see that He manifests Himself only to a few chosen people, as befits God's way of teaching about Himself in a manner that enters the world in humility and love rather than in power and proof.

For his part, von Balthasar argues that contemplation touches upon the historical credibility of Jesus' Resurrection (and other Christian claims) at an even deeper level, one that requires grace. He proposes that ultimately, the credibility of Jesus' Resurrection rests upon whether we contemplatively perceive that this "truth in person" is Divine Love, completely outside our human ability to invent because our fallen and finite love cannot embrace difference and surrender in the supreme way that this Divine Love does.[80] When we see this utterly self-surrendering Love, we enter into the contemplative friendship or fellowship with "truth in person" that

Aquinas describes, and we understand how (as Aquinas says) Christ's Resurrection reveals perfect goodness and perfect Divine justice and love. When we lack the love needed to contemplate this Divine Love, the historical arguments in favor of Jesus' Resurrection will be impeded by our empirical sense of the seemingly absolute power of death. But when Love incarnate moves us with its beauty and glory, we respond in love and contemplate Jesus' Resurrection as the truth of Love.

With regard to the credibility of Jesus' Resurrection, Ratzinger is right that when we contemplate Jesus as depicted in the Gospels, we see the canonical coherence of this portrait, which is itself testimony to the historicity of Jesus' Resurrection. Contemplating Jesus shows us other evidences of the historicity of His Resurrection, and so supernatural faith and love are not requisite for becoming aware of the truth of Jesus risen. But von Balthasar is right that it is our graced perception of radical Divine Love in Jesus Christ that assures us most decisively that Jesus is, indeed, risen from the dead and wills to draw all things into His self-surrendering love. Ultimately, therefore, Aquinas is right not only that contemplation is fueled by love, but also that the contemplation of Jesus Christ is the contemplation of "truth in person." As St. John Paul II urges priests and seminarians in *Pastores Dabo Vobis*, "Do not be afraid to open your minds to Christ the Lord who is calling. Feel his loving look upon you and respond enthusiastically to Jesus when he asks you to follow him without reserve."[81]

NOTES

1. Joseph Ratzinger, *Homilies at a First Mass: Joseph Ratzinger's Gift to Priests*, ed. Emery de Gaál, trans. David Augustine (Omaha, NE: IPF Publications, 2016), 51.

2. Ibid., 52-53.

3. John Paul II, *Pastores Dabo Vobis* (1992), Vatican trans. (Boston, MA: St. Paul Books & Media, 1992), sec. 18.

4. See Reza Aslan, *Zealot: The Life and Times of Jesus of Nazareth* (New York: Random House, 2013), xix.

5. Ibid., 174.

6. John Paul II, *Pastores Dabo Vobis*, sec. 49.

7. See, for example, the observations of Jacques Maritain, *Distinguish to Unite: or The Degrees of Knowledge*, trans. from the 4th French edition under the supervision of Gerald B. Phelan (Notre Dame, IN: University of Notre Dame Press, 1995), 348-49, 360. See also, for a perspective rooted in the Desert Fathers and applied to contemporary life, Thomas Merton, *New Seeds of Contemplation* (Boston: Shambhala, 2003).

8. Donald Haggerty, *Contemplative Provocations* (San Francisco: Ignatius Press, 2013), 19.

9. David Bentley Hart, *The Beauty of the Infinite: The Aesthetics of Christian Truth* (Grand Rapids, MI: Eerdmans, 2003), 329.

10. Hans Urs von Balthasar, *Love Alone Is Credible*, trans. D. C. Schindler (San Francisco: Ignatius Press, 2004). This short book sums up the central argument made by Hans Urs von Balthasar, *The Glory of the Lord: A Theological Aesthetics*, vol. 1: *Seeing the Form*, trans. Erasmo Leiva-Merikakis (San Francisco: Ignatius Press, 1982).

11. For this point, see also Jean Levie, S.J., *Sous les yeux de l'incroyant*, 2nd ed. (Paris: Desclée, 1946).

12. Thomas Aquinas, *Summa Theologicae* II-II, q. 180, a. 2.

13. Ibid., ad 2.

14. Ibid., ad 3.

15. II-II, q. 180, a. 3.

16. See ibid., ad 4.

17. II-II, q. 180, a. 4.

18. II-II, q. 180, a. 4.

19. Ibid., ad 3.

20. II-II, q. 180, a. 4, ad 3.

21. See 2 Corinthians 12:2-4.

22. Aquinas, II-II, q. 180, a. 5.

23. II-II, q. 180, a. 5, ad 2.

24. See II-II, q. 180, a. 7, ad 1.

25. See II-II, q. 180, a. 7; I-II, q. 31, a. 5.

26. II-II, q. 180, a. 7, ad 1. See Jacques and Raïssa Maritain, *Liturgy and Contemplation*, trans. Joseph W. Evans (New York: P. J. Kenedy & Sons, 1960), 51.

27. II-II, q. 180, a. 7 and ad 3.

28. See II-II, q. 188, a. 6, *sed contra*; Aquinas, *Commentary on the Gospel of John: Chapters 6-12*, trans. Fabian Larcher, O.P. and James A. Weisheipl, O.P., ed. Daniel A. Keating and Matthew Levering (Washington, D.C.: Catholic University of America Press, 2010), sec. 1510, p. 232.

29. Thomas Aquinas, *Summa Contra Gentiles*, Book I, ch. 1, trans. Anton C. Pegis, F.R.S.C. (Notre Dame: University of Notre Dame Press, 1975).

30. Ibid.

31. Ibid.

32. *Summa Contra Gentiles* Book I, ch. 2.

33. Cited in II-II, q. 23, a. 1, *sed contra*.

34. See 1 Corinthians 1:9.

35. Aquinas, *Summa Theologicae* III, q. 40, a. 1, ad 3. See also III, q. 37, a. 1, obj. 2 and elsewhere in the *tertia pars*.

36. III, q. 1, a. 1.

37. See Thomas Joseph White, O.P.'s brilliant and constructive *The Incarnate Lord: A Thomistic Study in Christology* (Washington, D.C.: Catholic University of America Press, 2015).

38. Aquinas, *Summa Theologicae* III, q. 46, a. 3.

39. See III, q. 46, a. 3.

40. III, q. 53, a. 1.

41. Aquinas, *Commentary on the Gospel of John: Chapters 13-21*, trans. Fabian Larcher, O.P. and James A. Weisheipl, O.P., ed. Daniel A. Keating and Matthew Levering (Washington, D.C.: Catholic University of America Press, 2010), sec. 1886.

42. III, q. 73, a. 5.

43. In this regard, Ratzinger directs attention to John P. Meier's historical-critical study of Jesus as "in many respects a model of historical-critical exegesis, in which the significance and the limits of the method emerge clearly" (Joseph Ratzinger/Pope Benedict XVI, *Jesus of Nazareth: From the Baptism in the Jordan to the Transfiguration*, trans. Adrian J. Walker [New York: Doubleday, 2007], 366). See also Joseph Ratzinger/Pope Benedict XVI, *Jesus of Nazareth: Part Two: Holy Week, From the Entrance into Jerusalem to the Resurrection*, trans. Vatican Secretariat of State (San Francisco: Ignatius Press, 2011), xv.

44. Ratzinger, *Jesus of Nazareth*, xi.

45. Ibid., xix.

46. Ibid., xxiii.

47. Ibid.

48. Ibid., xxii. See also Philippians 2:6-11.

49. Ratzinger, *Jesus of Nazareth*, xxi.

50. Ibid., xxiii.
51. Ratzinger, *Jesus of Nazareth: Part Two*, xv.
52. Ibid., xvi.
53. Ibid., xvii.
54. See ibid., 241.
55. Ibid., 245.
56. Ibid., 268.
57. Ratzinger, *Jesus of Nazareth: Part Two*, 272.
58. Ibid., 275.
59. Aquinas, *Summa Contra Gentiles*, Book I, ch. 1.
60. Von Balthasar, *Love Alone Is Credible*, 5. See Augustine, *On Christian Doctrine*, trans. D. W. Robertson, Jr. (New York: Macmillan, 1958), III. xv.23, p. 93; Blaise Pascal, *Pensées*, trans. Honor Levi, ed. Anthony Levi (Oxford: Oxford University Press, 1995), 85, sec. 329.
61. Von Balthasar, *Love Alone Is Credible*, 31.
62. Ibid., 38, 41.
63. Ibid., 51.
64. Ibid., 53.
65. Ibid., 56-57.
66. Ibid., 73.
67. Ibid., 79. See von Balthasar, *Seeing the Form*, 31, 76-77, 174, 209, 421, 466, 533, 538, 545, 553, 591, 618.
68. Von Balthasar, *Love Alone Is Credible*, 82.
69. Ibid., 83.
70. Ibid., 86.
71. Ibid., 89.
72. Ibid., 93.
73. Ibid., 101.
74. Ibid., 102. See Anselm's argument for God's existence in his *Proslogion*: Anselm, *Monologion* and *Proslogion*, trans. Thomas Williams (Indianapolis, IN: Hackett, 1996).
75. Von Balthasar, *Love Alone Is Credible*, 108.
76. Ibid., 109.
77. Ibid.
78. Ibid., 122.
79. Ibid., 127.
80. As shown by the encyclical *Deus Caritas Est*, Ratzinger likewise affirms this emphasis. See Pope Benedict XVI, *Deus Caritas Est*, Vatican trans. (Boston, MA: Pauline Books & Media, 2006).
81. John Paul II, *Pastores Dabo Vobis*, sec. 82.

Clarifications on the Notion of Religious Experience

Donald Haggerty

In a time of waning faith and growing indifference to religious practice, the question can be raised whether it is possible to speak at all today of a religious experience of the transcendent and the sacred. Has authentic religious experience of God disappeared, relegated to a rare and esoteric claim? The truth cannot be so extreme; yet who can deny that the diminishment of a religious sense has intensified notably in recent decades? Many factors have contributed in the current era to the widespread loss of a sense of religious mystery and of the transcendent, without which religion is reduced, at best, to an ethical proposal for right-living. The failure of serious Catholic catechesis among young people, for instance, has not just limited knowledge of the faith; it has impeded attraction for religious mystery. It has also left young people vulnerable to the onslaught of technological dependency. The societal obsession with technological diversion, with immediate and rapid information, with self-absorption in the gratifications of impulse, is a debilitating trend that cannot but undermine an openness to transcendent mystery. Christian religious experience implies, necessarily, an engagement in faith with revealed truths and the invisible, transcendent mystery of God. It cannot be accessed, as it were, simply by the proximity of a smartphone or a computer screen. This dilemma of a collapse in the sense of transcendent mystery has long been problematic in Western culture. Louis Dupré, for example, wrote in 1998:

> In the present situation, the very reality of the transcendent is at stake, more than its specific conceptualization. The very possibility of a relation to the transcendent in the modern world has come under fire. Theology in the past could count on some *direct* experience of the sacred. Such an experience can no longer be taken for granted. . . . The "experience of the sacred" . . . can no longer be considered normative of the religion of our time.[1]

These remarks give reason to reaffirm the essential importance and possibility of a religious experience of transcendent mystery and of God. The conviction of a Christian believer is not simply an act of faith without repercussions for personal life. It ought to lead to the lifelong quest for a personal encounter with the God who has revealed Himself in Jesus Christ. Authentic faith cannot be separated from an essential drive to seek the experience of God. The necessity of prayer and silence and some detached solitude open to God is essential to this experience of God. These are objective conditions that foster religious awareness. They are personal choices that must be made if we are to discover the reality of God with some depth of experiential faith. Yet, for many people, the very notion of religious experience seems confined to a subjective category and inherently resistant to objective confirmation. What exactly does it mean, then, to speak of religious experience as a Christian believer?

This question of religious experience was well-stated in a preface to the 1908 French edition of William James's classic work *The Varieties of Religious Experience*: "Fundamentally, what is this special experience that is described as religious experience? Is it no more than a purely subjective state, or is it a genuine communication with a being different and distinct from the conscious subject himself?"[2] These questions introduce the problem of religious experience in the starkest manner. As Christian believers, we reject a description of religious experience as a purely subjective state. Nonetheless, the problem remains to address the conditions and parameters for a soul's experience of God in this life. At the higher end of this spectrum of experiences of God may be so-called mystical experiences. It is a mistake, however, to confine the notion of an experience of God to rare, exalted states. At a more basic level is the Christian experience of the believer who may not be favored with extraordinary graces but who, nonetheless, by the nature of grace, is invited by faith to seek God and His will and to pursue a serious life of prayer. The experience of God cannot be separated from some determined quest for His presence in a life of prayer.

The life of interior prayer can be viewed as the most essential activity in this effort. At the same time, it is in the interior realm of prayer, by the nature of its subjectivity, that the question of an experience of God demands caution. This is especially true when one considers that the striving for God in prayer has a certain finality in the contemplative experience of prayer. God giving Himself in love to the soul is one way to describe the essential dynamic of grace taking place in contemplative prayer. Yet, what exactly this experience entails for a soul undergoing it requires careful understanding. A soul enjoying contemplative prayer, according to the most reliable treatments of it in the Catholic spiritual tradition, is granted an experience of God that is restricted and constrained, in one sense, and yet in real contact with God Himself in the Holy Trinity.

Already we can see, perhaps, a hint of the dilemma of religious experience. It involves a human subjectivity in relation to God and, for that reason, enters the realm of an encounter with nothing ultimately comparable in human experience, even if there are certain analogies between human relationships and the soul's relations with God. There is a certain unknowable element at the very heart of religious experience, due to the nature of God; and, indeed, this element of mystery is integral to relations between a soul and God. God is ultimate Other, the infinite mystery of being, infinite love in His ultimate transcendence. Yet He is known to us, accessible to our desire and our longing, making Himself known as a real presence, most particularly in the Sacrament of His love in the Eucharist. The mystery of God and the human experience of God encounter each other most sublimely in our contact with the holy disguise of the Sacred Host.

With these considerations in mind, I intend initially to examine some pertinent remarks of Jean Mouroux on religious experience from his 1955 book *The Christian Experience*, while allowing some of Jacques Maritain's writing to become an interlocutor to this discussion. An initial effort will be to clarify the place of affectivity in religious experience. I will then show, primarily through Maritain's insights, the

importance of an apophatic awareness for a healthy understanding of religious experience, and its role in tempering any
imbalance toward predominantly affective interpretations of
the nature of religious experience.

For a Christian believer, the doctrinal proposition of
God communicating Himself is a core truth of a revealed
religion. Religion, for us, is fundamentally a personal relationship with a God who has spoken and revealed Himself in
Jesus Christ the Logos, who ideally becomes, because He
is personal and has assumed a human nature, an object of
adoration and of love. From a Christian perspective, religious
experience derives immediately, as Mouroux writes, from
"the indissoluble relationship of adoration and love—the two
attitudes being mutually involved in each other, impregnat-
ing each other and together producing the act that lies at
the heart of all religion—prayer."[3] Religious experience, in
short, is the experience of a person in contact with a personal
God known in Jesus Christ. It is the act, as Mouroux writes,
"through which man becomes aware of himself in relation
to God."[4] These words remind us how central to Christian
religious experience is a regular contact, meditative and reflec-
tive, with the words of the Gospels. The Gospels expose to
us the face of God Himself in Jesus Christ. The consistent
reading and re-reading of the Gospels places us in a holy
proximity to the presence of God's voice and actions. In the
person of Jesus of Nazareth, we gaze on the limitless mystery
of God Himself.

Christian religious experience, while always returning to a
source in a God who has personally communicated Himself,
can also be described as an encounter with the mystery of the
holy. This word "holy" may lack precision in a philosophical

discussion but expresses well the mystery contained in God, a mystery of numinous holiness never properly fathomed, never reduced to a manageable conceptual understanding, yet someone of infinite magnitude who draws the soul precisely by His unknowability and who elicits a spirit of adoration. God is a Trinity of three Persons, a being of self-communicating love among Persons, and we cannot but prostrate ourselves before this holy mystery. As Mouroux writes, "a clearly conceived God could never be anything more than an idea, and therefore a nothingness, whereas the end of the religious relationship is necessarily mysterious by its very nature."[5] The heart of this mystery is the infinite difference that separates the holy nature of God from the human creature, the infinite distance that confronts our soul in turning our gaze toward God, the truth of Divine otherness, absolutely unlike any created reality. Contact with God necessarily means encounter with the vast abyss that separates Creator from creature. For Mouroux, the religious reality toward which we creatures turn is "abysmal" by definition. From this awareness rooted in the otherness of God arises a proper sense in the human person of his own nothingness, which is a religious perception, an integral element in religious experience, and necessary for a true relationship with God. "Only when this absolute nothingness is realized," Mouroux writes, "can religious experience take place."[6]

The absoluteness of Divine transcendence is never a truth in isolation. In Christianity, Divine transcendence cannot stand apart from a further reality, which is that God does communicate to souls and does make His presence known to those who seek Him. In this sense, Christian religious experience displays an essentially paradoxical element. The mystery of God remains intact, unbreachable, His fullness of truth beyond our grasp and experience; and yet, the human person experiences advances from God—solicitations from God, as it were—drawing the heart and soul in grace. Religious experience, in this sense, entails the consciousness of an appeal from a personal God speaking mysteriously to the unique life that is our own, inviting a freely offered submission. The appeal felt by the human person to submit to God involves always a certain contact proffered by God to our soul. This contact, essential to religious experience, affirms the reality of God as a personal presence who has made Himself to some degree accessible, open to encounter, even while concealed in transcendent mystery. If a human person responds to this contact initiated by God in grace and offers his or her submission to a personal God, the act of submission not only establishes relationship with God, but also reveals the deeper truth of self. And this latter discovery is, likewise, at the heart of religious experience. As Mouroux writes, "I reach to the truth of my being by submitting myself to God. . . . I give myself to God, but I am also someone who is given to himself by God. . . . In the religious act my centre becomes God, and this is the essential paradox of religious experience."[7] The paradox here is the Gospel's paradox. We discover the truth of ourselves only by giving ourselves to God.

Maritain's thinking on religious experience is more than compatible with these emphases. Indeed, Maritain strikes a high, eloquent note on this subject even in the context of his philosophical discussions. For example, in a long passage capturing an essential truth of the repercussion on self-awareness that ensues from the serious pursuit of God, he writes in *Existence and the Existent*:

Religion is essentially that which no philosophy can be: a relation of person to person with all the risk, the mystery, the dread, the confidence, the delight, and the torment that lie in such a relationship. . . . If God exists, then not I, but He is the centre; and this time not in relation to a certain particular perspective, like that in which each created subjectivity is the centre of the universe it knows, but speaking absolutely, and as transcendent subjectivity to which all subjectivities are referred. At such time I can know both that I am without importance and that my destiny is of the highest importance. I can know this without falling into pride, know it without being false to my uniqueness. Because, loving the divine Subject more than myself, it is for Him that I love myself, it is to do as He wishes that I wish above all else to accomplish my destiny; and because, unimportant as I am in the world, I am important to Him; not only I, but all the other subjectivities whose loveableness is revealed in Him and for Him and which are henceforth, together with me, a *we*, called to rejoice in His life.[8]

Despite this strong affirmation of personal relations with a transcendent God, another issue arises in addressing the matter of religious experience. Any valid notion of religious experience has to confront the question of contact with a presence irreducible to a finite, contingent encounter. The presence of God as experienced by a soul cannot be a naked contact with the fullness of God. It is a mediated presence that God offers, a presence by way of instrumental signs, a contact through the mediating operation of the theological virtues and of the gifts of the Holy Spirit. Since God is manifested as a mediated presence, there are difficulties for a human subjectivity to know that a true contact with God is taking place. The possibility of contact with the presence of God flows out of the religious experience itself, an experience of subjective orientation, which implies the dilemma of confirming its own objective validity. This uncertainty raises the question of affective experience as an objective medium for confirming any true contact of a soul with the presence of God. By its nature, affectivity seems to be a source of ambiguity in evaluating the legitimacy of religious experience. We turn now to address that question.

It is inevitable that religious experience will be accompanied, at times, by states of feeling. But religious affectivity is not without a potential for self-deception; and in part, this is due to the bodily link to feeling states. God is spirit, utterly transcendent, while we are composite creatures of body and soul, and therein lies an openness to possible error on the basis of misreading our own capacity for an experience of God, especially in prayer. By their nature, strong feelings in prayer enhance subjective conviction, which can be problematic if a person is convinced by an emotional state that God is communicating directly or that His presence is being felt, a conclusion that, in some cases, may be presumptuous and erroneous. Affective states, undeniable perhaps in their subjective intensity, require a sober response—not to dismiss them outright as necessarily misleading but to temper their appeal as a reliable measure of religious experience. The danger here is not the fact of emotion in religious experience, but of a misinterpretation of affectivity, the tendency to identify the validity of an experience of God with an experiential element in human life that is not a sound compass for examining relations between a soul and God. It is all too easy for us to judge a proximity of God to the soul or, on the other hand, a distance of God from the soul, by what is felt or not felt of God's presence. Yet those feelings do not transcend our bodily nature. On the contrary, they are rooted in bodily nature. The notion of a felt presence of God is an experience always within a private consciousness, a consciousness never removed from a constitutive insertion in a bodily human nature. A certain detachment from feelings and an ongoing purification of feeling are necessary, lest emotion induce certitudes about God and His presence to the soul that may lack objective truth.

This problem of assigning excessive value to feelings is, in part, to transfer certain experiential elements of Christian *mystical* experience to the ordinary life of a Christian believer. Mystical experience and higher contemplative experience do induce a consciousness of Divine action toward a soul. The soul's passivity in this experience, receptive toward an action felt as initiated from God, is combined with a consent and a collaboration on the part of the soul. The consciousness of suffering Divine love, the *pati divina*, is a classic description of authentic mystical experience. The phrase clearly implies a felt action of God suffered by the soul. With the exception of the higher graces of mystical experience, however, it cannot be said that faith and love necessarily produce empirical effects within consciousness. The religious experience of a Christian believer is essentially to possess a certitude that God is active within a life, but without any immediate felt perception of Divine presence or of communion with God. There is no necessary affective accompaniment to the act of faith.

Furthermore, the action of grace is normally imperceptible in the ongoing progression of a spiritual life. The absence of so-called spiritual feelings can be as common as their enjoyment. To wait habitually, on the other hand, for a feeling of grace, for affective inspiration, as a catalyst to actions is to risk an inertia in Christian living, a withdrawal from the active, sometimes uncertain pursuit of God's will that our Christian faith demands of us. When feelings do have a source in grace, they are an instrument that God, on occasion, uses to compel a response to His will. They are a means to a further end; but as a means, they disappear with the passing of time. The changeability of affective states in the interior life, showing endless alternations between fervor and distaste in the spiritual life, consolation and aridity, points to their instrumental use by God. Certainly, these varying affective states are not to be taken as a sign of God's arbitrariness toward the human soul, as though periods of His attentiveness to the soul might shift suddenly and without reasonable cause to periods of ignoring the soul. Much more realistic would be an acceptance that feelings must ultimately be transcended in times of fervor, and sacrificed in times of absence and vacuity. The soul's pursuit of God in an increasingly purer manner has always implied, in classical Catholic spirituality, a diminishment of self-conscious attention to any spiritual enjoyments God may extend to a soul in this life.

The problem of affectivity in religious experience is largely, then, one of insight and discernment. Affective states are psychological experiences necessarily rooted in subjectivity. Whether, at the same time, they are indicative of supernatural action proceeding from God is, perhaps, impossible to answer immediately. Grace is confirmed best by the actions that ensue from it. Relegating feelings undergone in prayer, or absent from prayer, to a secondary importance allows a proper subordination of feeling to observable virtue. Otherwise, an empiricist understanding of the operation of grace is likely to provoke imbalance within the soul, especially in the examination of prayer, as it turns to a dependency on an affective measure as the confirmation of Divine grace. The other primary objection to any excessive attention to affective states as a measure of relationship with God is the reflexive turn on self that inevitably ensues from this tendency. To the degree they are considered indicative of relations with God, affective states become sought after or introspectively examined in a manner that removes a soul from a selfless turning of interior focus toward God.

Maritain offered a fine warning in this regard in his short treatise *Prayer and Intelligence.* There, he denounced what he called "the most pernicious of vices," by which he meant a vice particular to souls serious about prayer, namely, "the reflex action of the mind, the tendency to come back on ourselves," precisely during the time of prayer. He writes:

> If we look at ourselves instead of looking at God, if we tighten our heart in order to scrutinize the state of our soul and take stock of our petty progress, if we leave our prayer in order to find out if it is good, or abandon our "quietude to see if it is really quiet" (St. Francis de Sales) . . . we lose the whole fruit of our spiritual life, we wander disquieted instead of entering into peace, we take the risk of numberless illusions.[9]

These words are pertinent especially to the danger of a self-centered attention to affective experience in prayer. The proper dynamic of prayer is oriented toward self-forgetfulness, a diminishment of any tendency to self-observation.

A strong emotion toward God that leads to a self-absorbed enjoyment of delight would be clearly contradictory to the movement of grace.

A consideration perhaps helpful to this problem of affectivity as a coveted element in religious experience is to note the possibility of a spiritual desire for God that is quite distinct from any affective experience of emotion. This state of desire for God, while difficult to measure, is conditioned by the soul's submission to God. Once a definitive response is made to God, the soul becomes subject to the gradual awakening of unlimited, inexhaustible spiritual desire. If the turn to God in submission is a profound one, the result for the soul will be an abiding condition of need for God, the soul perpetually drawn now in a movement toward God. This state of desire for God is a much more reliable measure of authentic religious experience than the interludes of particular drama that may touch affective experiences in prayer.

Moreover, once a soul arrives at a state of an abiding hunger for God, the infinite distance that separates God and the soul becomes a provocation to the soul, inducing it to search for ways to lessen this distance. Religious experience, in one sense, is to live an unappeased aspiration to reduce this distance, never succeeding in this effort, yet ceaselessly turned in the direction of a God who, once He has revealed Himself indubitably, may not seem to approach any closer to the soul. It is in this sense, on the very personal level of relations with God, that the Christian religious experience is apophatic in principle: our ignorance of God is impossible to overcome, and our possession of God remains, at best, a hope, always still unrealized. As Mouroux writes:

God is never discovered, in the strict sense of the word;
and the more we enter into the mystery of him, the more
we know him as someone essentially unknown, and each
day, by the power of that negative affirmation which
alone can give us being here below, we are taken further
and further beyond all that is clear and distinct and
consciously perceived. God is never *possessed*, in the strict
sense of the word, because he is not grasped in himself,
and consequently the more nearly he is approached the
more he is taken hold of as somebody absent, a presence
that is always slipping away, a "beyond" sustaining the
whole experience but never to be identified with it.[10]

Religious experience, in other words, is sustained only in
the continual search for God and His presence. It is a presence both ineluctably elusive and increasingly compelling to
any soul serious in its pursuit of God. Any claim of religious
experience must, therefore, reflect this dynamic orientation
of seeking God despite an elusive hiddenness in God.

The human person's awareness of a certain impotence
before the mystery of God is, perhaps surprisingly, a propi-
tious realization, advancing the soul's engagement with the
truth of God, conveying, by a richer encounter with what
is known, a deeper truth of God. As Maritain writes in *The
Degrees of Knowledge*, "This is not to say that He remains
unknown to us. Rather, He is known by us, He Himself is
known, but as remaining unknown."[11] In other words, a very
real knowledge of God is present in the awareness of an
insurmountable incomprehension in regard to the One who
is sought. Precisely as a realization of ignorance, the inaccessibility of the mystery in God can be pondered in itself
as a knowledge, steeping the intellect in a truth that will be

more intensively experienced under the effect of contemplative graces. There are decided benefits for the life of prayer in this "brushing up against" the facticity of God's absolute transcendence. For the reality of Divine transcendence is a relational notion. While it does not reveal anything of what God is in Himself, it does identify a quality of the Divine relationship with the soul seeking to know Him. Any experience of the Divine presence, even in elevated states of mystical union, occurs only within the darkened enclosure of blinded states of human unknowing. It can only be received as a transient encounter with a reality always reaching beyond human comprehension.

In the eternal actuality of the Divine "I am," God will always remain absolute Other, exceeding the immediate grasp of any particular act of human knowing, including any kind of mystical experience of God's presence to the soul. Maritain could be eloquent in writing on this subject, even within a context of philosophical discussion:

> This sovereign personality is at once that which removes Him most from us—the inflexible infinite confronting my mere manhood—and brings us closest to Him, for incomprehensible Purity has a countenance, a voice, and has set me face to face before It, that I may speak to Him and He respond. The light of His countenance is sealed upon us.[12]

Inasmuch as it is, above all, a relational notion, the transcendence of God signifies, then, not that God is unapproachable, rather, that He is approachable only in a certain manner, through a dissatisfaction that purifies the human person offering to God a submission of soul to Him. God is

known only by a love that leaves the Divine reality perpetually unknown in any way that can be permanently satisfying.
Christian religious experience, in other words, is at a certain
summit when it is an experience of the impossibility of
overcoming the essential inaccessibility contained in the
Divine mystery, precisely because He is known only through
love. The impossibility of overcoming an essential ignorance
before the Divine mystery will only inflame desire for an
immolating union with the God who is known only by a love
that leaves His Divine reality perpetually unknown in any
way that would satisfy the intellect. It is this superior manner
of approaching God that contemplative grace provides. The
unitive, connaturalizing effect of supernatural love depends,
in part, on a renunciation of all desire to know in a narrowly
conceptual manner so that the soul may be disposed for a
union of love with One who remains known only through
love. The early pages of Maritain's *The Degrees of Knowledge*
insist on the superiority of such a knowledge by love:

> It is clear, then, that although we can be given a
> knowledge of God, not *sicuti est*, that is, by His essence
> and in vision, but at least in accordance with the very
> transcendence of his Deity, that is, by making use of
> a mode of knowing appropriate to the object known,
> such a knowledge cannot possibly be obtained in a
> purely intellectual way. . . . We must pass through love.
> Love alone, and I am speaking of supernatural love,
> can effect this overreaching. Here below, intellect can
> enter the realm that lies beyond all method only by
> a renunciation-of-knowing in which God's Spirit, by
> making use of the connaturality of charity and the effects
> produced in affection by Divine Union, grants the soul

a loving experience of that very being which no notion approximates or can approximate.[13]

We might say, therefore, that the incapacity to comprehend God is a salutary note for religious experience. An initial frustration in this regard can give way to a fruitful acceptance of this blindness of the soul toward God. The mystery of Divine transcendence can be experienced in contemplation as a "place" of concealment hiding the ineffable personal presence of God. The transformed mode of knowing occurring in a contemplative response to God discovers the nearness, the proximity of the Divine presence, precisely in that concealment. Hiddenness is the mode of presence, as it were, of the God who is ever transcendent to the soul encountering Him. The very heart of Christian religious experience is in this truth. In his treatment of contemplative experience in *The Degrees of Knowledge*, Maritain quotes the striking advice of St. John of the Cross in *The Spiritual Canticle*, words that are particularly significant for a discussion of the religious experience of God:

> Seek Him ever as one hidden, for you exalt God immensely and approach very near Him when you consider Him higher and deeper than anything you can reach . . . never desire satisfaction in what you understand about God, but in what you do not understand about Him. Never stop with loving and delighting in your understanding and experience of God, but love and delight in what is neither understandable nor perceptible of Him. Such is the way . . . of seeking Him in faith. However surely it may seem that you find, experience, and understand God, you must, because He is inaccessible

and concealed, always regard Him as hidden, and serve Him who is hidden in a secret way."[14]

With these words of the Mystical Doctor in mind, we must affirm, in conclusion, that the progressive intensification of love between God and the soul never conquers this impenetrability of the Divine mystery. At times, the intellect of the contemplative may grope about among pockets of dim light, satisfying in themselves and offering the prospect of further discovery. But more and more, the contemplative soul must journey in faith through an unremitting darkness that pervades all contact with the living God. The truth of God as Divine Other, wholly veiled from sight, can be held only in the open palm of a hand that does not attempt to grip it. Descriptive paradoxes here cannot fully capture the experiential tensions intrinsic to a blind contact by loving adherence with the Divine mystery: a personal presence that precludes accessibility to the grasp of intellect, a knowledge by love that shrouds love from vision of the object of love, an intimacy that leaves the soul with more intense awareness of distance from the Beloved. If there is advancement in contemplative life, it is a progression in the intensity of love. It requires more and more surrender of the self, a willing loss of self, and of knowledge, too, and, eventually, a deeply embraced silence that must complement the blindness enclosing the contemplative's awareness of Divine presence.

A striking last statement of Maritain captures this importance of the surrender in love as the primary reality of religious experience:

The saints do not contemplate to know, but to love. They do not love for the sake of loving but for the love of

Him whom they love. It is for love of their first beloved,
God, that they aspire to that very union with God that
demands whilst they love themselves only for Him. For
them, the end of ends is not to bring exultation to their
intellect and nature and thus stop at themselves. It is to
do the will of Another, to contribute to the good of the
Good. They do not seek their own soul. They lose it; they
no longer possess it. If in entering into the mystery of
Divine filiation and becoming *something of God*, they gain
a transcendent personality, an independence and a liberty
which nothing in the world approaches, it is by forgetting
all else so that they do not live, but the Beloved lives
in them."[15]

As a last comment to close our discussion, we might
affirm that the effort to highlight and promote the rich
contemplative resources in the Catholic tradition would seem
an essential task in the current day. Not all Catholics, even
among priests and religious, are inclined to pursue the serious
personal engagement in spirituality that allows these resources
to come alive. But even if the tradition of Catholic spirituality
is not widely appreciated and studied, what must not happen
is that the study of Christian spirituality in its more advanced
treatments is relegated to irrelevance and then forgotten. The
recovery of a sense of transcendence is directly linked to a
reassertion of serious spirituality, at least in some quarters
of Catholic life; and this requires an element of study and
sacrificial pursuit. Sound spirituality tends to filter down
in a healthy manner to influence all who are exposed to
serious manifestations of it. We can expect that more serious approaches to a vocation, especially among priests and
religious, will follow as souls recognize the great adventure

of pursuing God and the open possibilities for personal experience that this quest implies. We conclude, therefore, with a listing of recommended texts that can aid and stimulate this quest.

St. John of the Cross—*The Collected Works*

St. Teresa of Avila—*The Way of Perfection* and *The Interior Castle*

Fr. Reginald Garrigou-Lagrange, O.P.—*The Three Ages of the Interior Life (2 Vols.)*

Fr. Marie-Eugène, O.C.D.—*I Want To See God* and *I Am a Daughter of the Church*

Fr. Thomas Dubay—*Fire Within*

Evelyn Underhill—*Mysticism*

Fr. Conrad de Meester, O.C.D.—*With Empty Hands*

Cardinal Robert Sarah—*The Power of Silence*

Fr. Walter Ciszek, S.J.—*He Leadeth Me*

Fr. Augustín Guillerand—*They Speak by Silences*

NOTES

1. Louis Dupré, *Religious Mystery and Rational Reflection* (Grand Rapids, MI: William B. Eerdmans, 1998), 142, 134.

2. William James, *The Varieties of Religious Experience* (New York: Mentor Books, 1958), 6.

3. Jean Mouroux, *The Christian Experience*, trans. George Lamb (New York: Sheed and Ward, 1955), 7.

4. Ibid., 15.

5. Ibid., 17.

6. Ibid.

7. Ibid., 19.

8. Jacques Maritain, *Existence and the Existent*, trans. Lewis Galantiere and Gerald B. Phelan (New York: Pantheon, 1948), 73, 75.

9. Jacques and Raïssa Maritain, *Prayer and Intelligence*, trans. Algar Thorold (New York: Sheed & Ward, 1943), 26.

10. Mouroux, *The Christian Experience*, 24.

11. Jacques Maritain, *The Degrees of Knowledge*, trans. under supervision of Gerald B. Phelan (New York: Charles Scribner's Sons, 1959), 237.

12. Ibid., 235.

13. Ibid., 14.

14. St. John of the Cross, *The Spiritual Canticle*, 1.12 in *The Collected Works of St. John of the Cross*, trans. Kieran Kavanaugh and Otilio Rodriguez (Washington, D.C.: ICS, 1979), 420.

15. Maritain, *The Degrees of Knowledge*, 10.

Letting Christ Take Flesh in a Culture of Unbelief: Joseph Ratzinger and Seminary Formation

Mary McCaughey

Introduction

In the context of a theological culture influenced by
the Enlightenment and the Reformation, Joseph Ratzinger
highlights that a reductive understanding of Christ and His
ministry has led to a reductive understanding of priesthood.
Hence, in an address to the World Synod of Bishops in 1990,
he explores Christ's identity and its Biblical roots to clarify the
theological foundations of priesthood in light of Tradition.
He highlights that the centrality of Christ's identity is His
relationship to the Father, His embodiment of the Father's
mission, and His call to return all to the Father.[1] Like Christ,
who acts from a power given to Him by His Father, and
like the Apostles, a priest acts not from his own power but
from that of Christ; and this is the basis of the Sacrament
of Ordination.[2]

The biblical basis of the apostolic ministry is to bring about reconciliation: communion with God and within the Christian community, as well as representing Christ's shepherding role.[3] Hence, Ratzinger highlights that fundamental to formation for priesthood is the fostering of a "deep personal relation with Christ."[4] Thus, he writes, "a presbyter ought to be a human being who knows Jesus intimately, if he has met him and learned to love him." He should be "a human being of prayer, one who is deeply 'spiritual,'" and he "should also learn from the mystery of Christ not to seek himself in his life or his own advancement."[5]

This emphasis on representing Christ and His ministry of salvation is for the ordained minister both a gift and a task supported by a relationship of prayer. These links are echoed in many Church documents on the priestly formation and ministry. *The Gift of the Priestly Vocation* points out that "the heart of spiritual formation is personal union with Christ, which is born of, and nourished in a particular way by prolonged and silent prayer."[6] The aim of spiritual formation is to nurture communion with God and others "in the friendship of Jesus" and with "an attitude of docility to the Holy Spirit."[7] The *Directory for the Life and Ministry of Priests* explains that the priest becomes "in the Church and for the Church, a real, living and faithful image of Christ the Priest, 'a sacramental representation of Christ, Head and Shepherd.'"[8] He is also "a minister of redemption," a "source of new life," and, thus, "an instrument of the new creation."[9]

Western Culture and the Ministry of Salvation:
The Separation of Faith and Reason and the Crisis of God

For Ratzinger, the culture that has led to such a reductive understanding of priesthood ignores cultic dimensions and removes all that is sacred. In his view, it draws its inspiration from selecting passages from St. Paul that associate priesthood and cult with "law" and with "works." The category of "priest" is now surpassed by the category of the "Gospel" and the "prophet."[10] Elsewhere, however, Ratzinger has deeply analyzed the roots of contemporary Western culture, its separation of faith and reason, and its resulting anthropology and theory of knowledge. These factors influence a certain understanding of priesthood and priestly formation that must be addressed and corrected in light of Tradition.

Joseph Ratzinger highlights the "positivist—and therefore anti-metaphysical character," of Western culture that entails "a mutilation of man if generalised."[11] The effect of Enlightenment thinking, influenced by universal reason, has also reduced reason's capacity to find objective universal truth to the ability to assemble empirically verifiable facts.[12] Faith is separated from reason and confined to the world of paradox and irrationality or, on the other hand, reduced to rationalism.[13] It is no longer seen as containing anything reasonable. It, thereby, "loses its capacity to explain and penetrate everyday life."[14] The legacy of the "faith alone" approach means that contemporary Western culture has now sanitized God, aiming to write Him out of history. As Ratzinger explains, the disappearance of the "concept of God itself follows in its wake,"[15] leading in practice to a crisis of "God," or a general disbelief among people in God's role in their lives.[16]

If, in contemporary thought, the Deist God of Kantian rationalism reigns supreme over the God of the Incarnation, this has implications for Church and priesthood. The idea that God is active in human lives—transforming them by the gift of salvation so that they become "new creatures" in

Christ and the Spirit—is the very foundation of the nature
of the Church as a sacrament of salvation to the world. It
is also the basis for the Christological and apostolic nature
of priesthood as a ministry of reconciliation and, thus, for
priestly identity and human, spiritual, intellectual, and pastoral
formation in the seminary.

Unfortunately, seminary formation has not emerged
unscathed from the separation of faith and reason and, thus,
a reductive view of priesthood, priestly ministry, and formation. Ratzinger points out that theological formation for
seminarians in Germany since the 1960s has been confined to
secular universities delivering a historical approach to theology that often ignores metaphysics and contains no influence
of faith and spirituality.[17] As a corrective to this, he highlights
the need at all times to integrate faith, reason, and spirituality,
"since loving him [Christ] means knowing him, a will ready to
undertake study which is careful and accurate is a sign of the
solidity of a vocation."[18] St. John Paul II similarly pointed out
in an address to Maynooth seminary in Ireland in 1979 that:

> theological learning, here as everywhere throughout the
> Church, is a reflection on faith, a reflection in faith. A
> theology which did not deepen faith and lead to prayer
> might be a discourse on words about God; it could not be
> a discourse about God, the living God, the God who is
> and whose being is *Love*.[19]

This multi-dimensional, integrated, and holistic approach
to seminary formation counteracts an Enlightenment anthropology and epistemology. It takes a Catholic approach to
knowledge theory. Such an approach is evident in *Pastores
Dabo Vobis*, which explains how theological formation is to

overcome a "purely abstract approach to knowledge," in favor of "that intelligence of heart which knows how to 'look beyond,'" since only then can a priest "communicate the mystery of God to people."[20]

For Ratzinger, faith draws the believer into a relationship with Christ through a contemplative purity of heart that engages both the heart and the intellect,[21] and this is the basis of theology. His theological epistemology is influenced by the theology of John Henry Newman,[22] as well as the personalistic theology of Romano Guardini.[23] For Ratzinger, central to the theological task is the theologian's relationship with the person of Christ. In the encyclical *Lumen Fidei*, written by Pope Benedict XVI to complete his trilogy on faith, hope, and love (and completed and promulgated by Pope Francis), he writes that theology is not "simply an effort of human reason to analyse [*sic*] and understand along the lines of the experimental sciences," since "God cannot be reduced to an object. He is a subject who makes himself known and perceived in an interpersonal relationship."[24] Faith also perfects reason in its operation to know truth. For Ratzinger, "right faith orients reason to open itself to the light which comes from God, so that reason, guided by love of the truth can come to a deeper knowledge of God."[25]

Faith, Reason, and Discernment of Culture

A Catholic approach to "knowing," where faith is connected to reason and spirituality, also means that faith cannot be proclaimed in a fideistic vacuum. This is evident in Ratzinger's proposal that the faithful be encouraged to enter into a growing dialogue with the *logos* where it exists as seeds of the word (*semina verbi*) in culture, other religions,

and philosophies.[26] Dialogue can highlight the reasonable
elements within both religion and culture, as well as the
irrational elements within both from which they need to be
purified. For Ratzinger, other religions should be interpreted
not as closed systems but in terms of how they bring salvation. This means to discern their elements based on to what
extent they bring human beings to seek the face of God and
His kingdom.[27] Only on the basis of the discernment can elements be found that are worthy of dialogue with Christianity,
a religion with roots in reason and *logos*. However, since, in
Christianity, *logos* is revealed as creative love, its distinctiveness
is not that it is connected just to reason, but that it brings
together faith, reason, and *life*. The Christian philosophy
gives to humanity an ethics of charity revealed in Christ and
not simply a truth that appeals to intellectual reason alone.[28]
Christians were always known by virtue of the distinctive love
or *caritas* that they showed to the poor, the suffering, and the
most vulnerable.[29]

For Ratzinger, since believers are tempted to uncertainty
just as unbelievers are continually tempted to faith, dialogue
with unbelievers is also possible and necessary. What believers
and unbelievers have in common is their humanity.[30] To show
how this works, later as Pope Benedict XVI, Ratzinger established the "Court of the Gentiles," inviting atheists to enter
into dialogue with Catholics on key topics to do with culture,
society, and anthropology.[31]

As Tracey Rowland points out, Ratzinger's understanding of the dialogue of faith with culture is to see culture
in the light of Christ and to critique it through this lens.
His approach has much in common with that of Hans
Urs von Balthasar and Henri De Lubac and differs from a

correlationist approach common after the Second Vatican Council and evident, for example, in the work of David Tracey or Kathryn Tanner.[32] For Ratzinger, faith gives the ability to distinguish what is true and constant from what is merely culturally relevant. The type of faith he advocates does not follow "the trends of fashion and the latest novelty" but is radically Christo-centric, "deeply rooted in friendship with Christ."[33] In an article written twenty years after the Second Vatican Council document *Gaudium et Spes*, he notes a certain approach to history and truth, writing:

> Certainly we cannot return to the past, nor have we any desire to do so. But we must be ready to reflect anew on that which, in the lapse of time, has remained the one constant. To seek it without distraction and to dare to accept, with joyful heart and without diminution, the foolishness of truth—this . . . is the task for today and for tomorrow: the true nucleus of the Church's service to the world, her answer to the "joy and hope, the grief and anguish of the men of our time" (*GS*, 903).[34]

For Ratzinger, then, faith gives the ability to discern what is true and constant in culture. Rooted in friendship with Christ, faith "opens human beings up to all that is good and at the same time gives a criterion by which to distinguish the true from the false, and deceit from truth."[35] In an insightful homily for the Feast of St. Henry, he explains how faith gives the gift of such an ability when he writes:

> Who can look through and beyond the mass of experiences and images, of ideologies and dominant opinions? . . . Only God can give this to us . . . Only God can create a pure vision for us; only he can liberate us

from the hopelessness of scepticism and grant us to see the truth through all the confusion. The pure vision is identical with the faith that tells us what is decisive and essential in the obscurity of the things of this world. But to keep the faith and so to see the right direction is today, as at all times, and perhaps more than in other times, a grace we must pray for.[36]

These reflections of Ratzinger on discernment of the culture through faith highlight the importance of the priest as a "man of discernment able to read the reality of human life in light of the spirit" emphasized in *The Gift of the Priestly Vocation*.[37] Since Pope Francis is a Jesuit, the concept of discernment is a familiar one to him; however, for one without his understanding of the Ignatian roots of discernment, his ideas on accompaniment can be misinterpreted. The idea of accompaniment in pastoral ministry put forward in *Amoris Laetitia* has given rise to an uneasiness and fear that it will lead to subjective interpretations in difficult pastoral situations. However, discernment accompanied by a spiritual director in the Ignatian tradition means always to seek to choose the will of God. This is only possible when the believer is rooted in a prayer relationship and communion with the Church; and in this way, subjective conformation to cultural trends opposed to Church teaching can be avoided.[38]

The importance of spiritual accompaniment for the seminarian and priest is vital and is the foundation for his ability to exercise that gift for others in ministry. The Ignatian spiritual tradition also provides a Christological context for the ministry of discernment. The Spiritual Exercises assist the seminarian to conform himself to Christ and to interpret life experience, events, and his prayer in the light of Christ and can be undertaken during seminary formation as a thirty-day retreat and again in shorter retreats during priesthood. St. Ignatius's "Principle and Foundation" provides insights into what in life brings one nearer to God and the goal to praise Him above all things. It also brings to light what might be a lesser good leading one further from that goal. The Ignatian "two standards" can strengthen the ability to distinguish between the "standard of Christ" and "the standard of the world." Values of the world rooted in individualism and autonomy such as pride, love of reputation, and desire for human respect contrast radically with the values of Christ such as humility, love of humiliation, and misunderstanding.[39] This "two standards" approach can be seen in Pope Francis's emphasis on the importance of humility for combating clericalism.[40] In an address to Italian seminarians, he says:

> Do not feel different from your peers, or that you are better than other people . . . If tomorrow you will be priests who live in the midst of the holy people of God, begin today to be young people who know how to be with everyone, who can learn something from every person you meet, with humility and intelligence.[41]

This clear division of values in the two standards might also help to interpret Pope Francis's hard-hitting first Christmas homily to the Curia, criticizing—among other qualities—rivalry, vainglory, and self-seeking.[42]

The key insights of Ignatian discernment are not merely techniques to be applied but are deeply Christocentric concepts belonging within the context of a personal friendship with Christ through following the Spirit. In this way, Ignatian spirituality complements Ratzinger's Christocentric emphasis in the spiritual life and can be strengthened by contemplative prayer, adoration, *lectio divina*, and the life-giving reception of the Sacraments.

Freedom of Autonomy and Freedom of Communion

Another feature of contemporary liberal culture is that it has cut itself off from its historical roots, detaching itself "from . . . the basic memory of mankind."[43] It values a progress that forever changes but neglects the past and contains no perennial wisdom or what Zygmunt Bauman describes as "liquid modernity."[44] Such a freedom without roots leads to a relativistic approach to social and moral norms that Peter Berger and Thomas Luckmann describe as "the constitution of social reality through subjective meanings" with roots in the thought of Schutz, Durkheim, Weber, and Marx's dialectics.[45]

As Ratzinger repeats often, a socially constructed view of the human being that neglects metaphysical foundations means that thinking "only practicably of what can be made, he [man] forgets to reflect on himself and the meaning of his existence."[46] It also leads to a false freedom that, as *Pastores Dabo Vobis* notes, "is lived out as a blind acquiescence to instinctive forces and to an individual's will to power."[47] The moral aim it proposes is, as Von Balthasar describes, that the human being grasp his freedom and "shape his own diameter."[48] In terms of morality, it inspires a relativism that "does not recognize anything as absolute and leaves as the ultimate measure only the measure of each one and his desires."[49]

For Ratzinger, faith is the opposite. It "does not belong to the relationship 'know-make,' which is typical of the

intellectual context of 'makability' thinking."[50] In the context
of the Sacrament of Priesthood, Ratzinger also explains that
sacramental thinking differs from makeability thinking. Sacramental thinking in view of priestly identity means "a human
being is in no way performing works which issue from natural
ability or talent . . . in addition no community can by its
decree promote a human being to this ministry."[51] He points
out, however, that the Sacrament of Orders does not mean
that in receiving his identity from Christ, a priest's humanity
is annihilated. Rather, through sharing in Christ's identity
through the Sacrament of Priesthood, his own humanity is
brought to perfection.[52] In Catholic tradition, as Ratzinger
highlights, grace perfects nature rather than destroys it; and,
thus, "we can only be truly 'creative' and also able to create, when we do it in unity with the Creator, the maker of
the world."[53]

Letting Christ Take Flesh: The Importance of Mary and Nuptial Fruitfulness

The seminarian's identity is found through entry into a
contemplative, participative life in the Trinity. In essence,
this is an entry into the mystery of the Church.[54] In a paper
on seminary formation, Cardinal Marc Ouellet explains that
through the Church as sacrament, the "freedom of autonomy" is corrected by "the freedom of communion, which the
grace of Christ has introduced into the world."[55] He writes:

> If the Church is the manifestation of Trinitarian
> communion for the salvation of the world, it follows
> that the Trinitarian relations must be reflected in the
> exchanges that the ecclesial community lives out at the

heart of its mission. The baptised and ordained ministers participate, each in their own way, in these relations.[56]

Understanding the Church as a sacrament of salvation rooted in the Trinitarian missions means recognizing how God continues to act in the world transforming human lives. Romano Guardini described the ecclesiological event of the Second Vatican Council as "the Church is awakening in people's souls."[57] In his last address to the Cardinals before his resignation, Pope Emeritus Benedict, commenting on this phrase from Guardini, links it to Mariology. Mary, as the one most transformed by God's grace through a relationship of faith and love with the persons of the Trinity, represents the Church. He writes that it means:

> The Church is alive; she grows and is reawakened in souls who—like the Virgin Mary—welcome the Word of God and conceive it through the action of the Holy Spirit; *they offer to God their own flesh.* It is precisely in their poverty and humility that they become capable of begetting Christ in the world today. Through the Church, the Mystery of the Incarnation lives on forever. Christ continues to walk through the epochs and in all places.[58]

The Mariological dimensions of the Church highlight that salvation is a gift to be received and a mystery to be entered into rather than manufactured. The "makeability" culture is radically opposed by the sign of Mary. Since divinity and humanity are first knitted together in her womb, the *Theotokos* is the great sign of the work of salvation, of grace and fruitfulness, revealed in an incomparable way. The great women of the Old Testament—Sarah, Rachel, Hannah, and

Elizabeth—who were barren and yet conceive through waiting on the Lord and His action, point figuratively to Mary, the Virgin, who paradoxically becomes Mother through grace.[59] This dynamic of fruitfulness by grace points to the character of the new creation represented by those within the body of Christ, the Church.

Secondly, the Mariological dimensions of Church highlight that salvation is transformative of intellectual, affective, bodily, and spiritual dimensions of the human being. Mary's life testifies to a truly existential and metaphysical freedom, rooted in union with God, unlike the freedom of autonomy so highly prized by contemporary culture. Both *Lumen Gentium* and *Redemptoris Mater* highlight that Mary's faith in God's work at each event of her life from the Annunciation to the Cross brings her into the freedom of communion with God and the ultimate fruitfulness of grace as Mother of the Church.[60] Von Balthasar highlights that at the Cross, she reaches the fullness of faith and shares the kenosis of Christ experiencing anabandonment by her Son (just as He experiences abandonment by the Father) so as to find a new existence in the order of grace.[61]

In Mary, faith is revealed not merely as a spiritual relationship understood gnostically as "other-worldly" but is connected to "being" through the category of "pathos."[62] She continues to safeguard the reality of the Incarnation, guarding the Church from any dualistic tendencies. Like her, the saints offer to God their own flesh, bringing about a physiological change in their bodies, opening them up so that they can go out of self ecstatically in love to others[63] and also be affected by others.[64] The prayer to the Trinity of Saint Elizabeth of the Trinity captures the all-embracing power of faith to transform the entire nature of the human being in body and soul. She calls on the Holy Spirit to "come down in me and reproduce in me, as it were, an incarnation of the word, that I may be to him a new humanity wherein he may renew his mystery."[65] Graham McAleer presents this dynamic expressed in a fruitful "nuptial body" in the life of St. Catherine of Siena. He writes:

> Her love for God has wounded Catherine, it has "crucified desire," and the prayerful unity of her sensuality and intellect has made her ecstatic. In this ecstacy [*sic*] she is made fecund . . . when she "clothes herself with truth," this transforms Catherine's sensuality into a nuptial body. Through the fecundity of her bridegroom, Christ, she conceives virtues, and herself drowned "in the gentle blood," her bridegroom helps her to give birth to her love of neighbour.[66]

Mary and the saints become for the seminarian a model of his nuptial identity.[67] The call to ministerial priesthood is also in harmony with the nuptial call of all in the common priesthood to self-gift and the offering of charity as explained in *Lumen Gentium*[68] and is linked to the Eucharist. The seminarian, as all the members of the Body of Christ, is to be wounded by His love manifested on the Cross which draws him out of self in love for others. In a particular way, he represents Christ as priest and the ministry of reconciliation and love. All baptized members of the Body are called to unite their daily sacrifices of love with the offering of Christ on the altar, the ultimate embodiment of love, under the form of bread and wine.[69] For Augustine, as Ratzinger explains, the Eucharist is not simply a mystical offering that is confined to the Eucharistic Liturgy itself but is one with the moral offering of the life of Christians in the charity they show to each other.[70] In the encyclical *Sacramentum Caritatis*, as Pope Benedict, he explains how Martyrdom in the history of the Church has "always been seen as the culmination of the new spiritual worship: 'Offer your bodies' (*Rom* 12:1)"[71] and charity as worship is connected to Christ's gift of self in the Eucharist. Just as Saint Ignatius of Antioch connected his coming martyrdom with the Eucharist,[72] the "Christian who offers his life in martyrdom enters into full communion with the Pasch of Jesus Christ and . . . becomes Eucharist with him."[73] In his formation for priesthood, the seminarian, in particular, is called to reflect on the connection between Eucharist, Christ, and self-giving. Hence, through continuously uniting himself to God in prayer, study, faith, and in the Sacraments and, in particular, through the Eucharist, he becomes increasingly affected by Christ, conformed to Him, and becomes as Elizabeth of the Trinity proclaims, "a praise of God's glory,"[74] which is the purpose of sacrifice and offering connected to priesthood.

This nuptial communion with Christ in the flesh is also to be understood as expressed by a life of fruitful celibacy. St. John Paul II explains, both marital love and continence are two expressions of conjugal love and fruitful forms of paternity or maternity[75]:

> the choice of virginity or celibacy for one's whole life
> . . . has acquired the significance of an act of nuptial
> love, that is, a nuptial giving of oneself for the purpose
> of reciprocating in a particular way the nuptial love of

the Redeemer. It is a giving of oneself understood as
renunciation, but made above all out of love.[76]

As *Pastores Dabo Vobis* explains, spiritually the seminarian
takes on the form of Christ the Bridegroom and becomes
ecstatically opened and fruitful for His Bride the Church.[77]
Pastoral ministry and communion with others in charity flow
from nuptial union with Christ as its source.[78] Vertical communion with Christ is essential for understanding the identity,
dignity, vocation, and mission of the priest at a horizontal
level "among the People of God and the world."[79] Ratzinger
explains how:

> one whose inner self knows Christ wishes to
> communicate also to others the personally experienced
> joy of redemption in the Lord. Pastoral work flows from
> this communion of love; even in trying circumstances it is
> nourished by this motivation and fulfils life.[80]

Principles of Seminarian Formation

Having examined these theological strands in Ratzinger,
we can now outline certain principles of formation. Firstly,
seminary formators are to assist seminarians live in deepest
friendship with Christ forged in the intimacy of faith, prayer,
and listening to the Spirit. Only this will enable them by grace
to truly represent Christ and His ministry. Pope Emeritus
Benedict XVI, quoting the words of Pope St Gregory the
Great on the necessary connection between the interior life
and ministry writes:

> What else are holy men but rivers which water the
> parched earth of carnal hearts? Yet . . . they would very

quickly be dried up unless they determine in their heart
to take care always to return to the place from which they
spring. For if they do not return inward to the heart and
bind themselves with chains in the love of their Creator's
wishes . . . their tongue grows dry. Rather do they return
inward always through love. And what they pour forth
publicly in work and speech, in secret they draw from
their fountain of love. For loving they learn what in
teaching they put forth" (Hom in Ez. Lib 1 hom V 16, PL
76, 828 B.)[81]

Secondly, formators are to emphasize that friendship with
Christ also provides the means to interpret culture through
the eyes of faith. Thus, seminarians will be able to recognize
the signs of the *logos* in the world rather than unconditionally
embracing all that culture has to offer. Formation challenges
the seminarian to follow the Paschal path of the Death and
Resurrection of Christ, inspiring a counter-cultural witness.
This, as Hans Urs von Balthasar explains in the *Moment of
Christian Witness*, has been the path trodden by every saint
who has "attempted to shape his life into a loving response to
the crucified Trinitarian love of God and thus placed himself
at the disposition of Jesus' work of establishing God's kingdom of love among men."[82]

Thirdly, formators can highlight that priestly identity is
linked to Mariology in that it is a gift of grace expressed in
nuptiality and fruitfulness. The seminarian's call has a nuptial
structure, and Mary becomes a model for the seminarian
that fruitfulness in charity and self-offering is possible only
through grace. It is this dynamic of graced fruitfulness which
is the core of the seminarian's spiritual and pastoral life. He
is to be fashioned by the Spirit to be a new creation in Christ

(2 Cor 5:17). Like Mary, he is to bring Christ to the world, "in his flesh," meaning through his entire life and existence. Like Christ, he is to live the Eucharistic offering of his Body (representing his life) in living sacrifice to God and for others. Living a fruitful faith, the seminarian will become a testimony to a faith that is real, active, and life-giving—not dualistic, mythological, and rationalistic—and will grow into the priestly sign that God is, indeed, "Emmanuel" forging a communion and love with and among His people.

Through a relationship with Christ fostered in prayer, seminarians are growing into a sign that Christ's work of healing reconciliation and salvation continues in the world through the Church, the Sacraments, and in its own particular way, through the Sacrament of Priesthood. The privilege and wonder of the call to priesthood, rooted in the priestly identity of Christ and His ministry of self-giving, reconciliatory love between God and man is to be central to seminarian formation. It is summed up in the words of the Curé of Ars: "The priest continues the work of redemption on earth. . . . If we really understood the priest on earth, we would die not of fright but of love. . . . The Priesthood is the love of the heart of Jesus."[83]

NOTES

1.   Joseph Ratzinger, "Biblical Foundations of Priesthood," *Communio* (Winter 1990): 620.

2.   Ibid.

3.   Ibid., 621.

4.   Ibid.

5.   Ibid., 626.

6.   Congregation for the Clergy, *The Gift of the Priestly Vocation, Ratio Fundamentalis Institutionis Sacerdotalis* 102, http://www.clerus.va/content/dam/clerus/Ratio%20Fundamentalis/The%20Gift%20of%20the%20Priestly%20Vocation.pdf (accessed June 10, 2017).

7.   Congregation for the Clergy, *The Gift of the Priestly Vocation*, 101, and see Second Vatican Council, *Presbyterorum Ordinis, Decree on the Ministry and Life of Priests* (1965), http://www.vatican.va/archive/hist_councils/ii_vatican_council/documents/vat-ii_decree_19651207_presbyterorum-ordinis_en.html, sec. 12 (accessed August 25, 2017).

8.   Congregation for the Clergy, *Directory for the Life and Ministry of Priests*, 1994, http://www.vatican.va/roman_curia/congregations/cclergy/documents/rc_con_cclergy_doc_31011994_directory_en.html (accessed October 11, 2017).

9.   Mauro Cardinal Piacenza and Celso Morga Iruzubieta, "Preface," *Directory for the Life and Ministry of Priests*, 2013 edition, sec. 5, http://www.clerus.org/clerus/dati/2013-06/13-13/Direttorio_EN.pdf (accessed October 25, 2017).

10.   Joseph Ratzinger, "Biblical Foundations of Priesthood," 618.

11.   Ratzinger, *Christianity and the Crisis of Cultures* (San Francisco: Ignatius Press, 2006), 40.

12.   Ibid., 35.

13.   Kant's portrayal of a rational religion is evident in *Religion within the Limits of Reason Alone* (New York: Harper, 1960).

14.   Joseph Ratzinger, *The Nature and Mission of Theology: Essays to Orient Theology in Today's Debates* (San Francisco: Ignatius, 1995), 21.

15.   Ibid.

16.   See Ratzinger, "The Ecclesiology of the Constitution on the Church, Vatican II, 'Lumen Gentium,'" in *L'Osservatore Romano*, [English Edition], no. 38 (Sept 2001): 5. See also, *Pilgrim Fellowship of Faith: The Church as Communion* (San Francisco: Ignatius, 2002), 124.

17.   Ratzinger, *The Nature and Mission of Theology*, 128.

18.   Ratzinger, "Biblical Foundations of Priesthood," 626.

19.   John Paul II, "Address of the Holy Father John Paul II to Priests, Missionaries, Religious Brothers and Sisters." St Patrick's College, Maynooth October 1, 1979, https://w2.vatican.va/content/john-paul-ii/en/

speeches/1979/october/documents/hf_jp-ii_spe_19791001_maynooth-religious-people.html (accessed July 10, 2017).

20. John Paul II, *Pastores Dabo Vobis* (1992), sec. 51.

21. Joseph Ratzinger, *A New Song for the Lord: Faith in Christ and Liturgy Today* (New York: Crossroad, 1997), 53.

22. See Benedict XVI. "Prayer Vigil on the Eve of the Beatification of Cardinal John Henry Newman, (Hyde Park, London, Sat September 18, 2010)," https://w2.vatican.va/content/benedict-xvi/en/speeches/2010/september/documents/hf_ben-xvi_spe_20100918_veglia-card-newman.html (accessed November 23, 2017).

23. As Benedict XVI says in *Deus Caritas Est*, sec. 1, being Christian "is the encounter with an event, a person." See *Deus Caritas Est*, God is Love, http://w2.vatican.va/content/benedict-xvi/en/encyclicals/documents/hf_ben-xvi_enc_20051225_deus-caritas-est.html (accessed September 2, 2017).

24. Francis, *Lumen Fidei* (2013), sec. 36, http://w2.vatican.va/content/francesco/en/encyclicals/documents/papa-francesco_20130629_enciclica-lumen-fidei.html (accessed November 15, 2017).

25. Ibid.

26. This approach to dialoguing with human truth wherever it is found is discussed by Ratzinger in *Truth and Tolerance* (San Francisco: Ignatius, 2004), in various sections. For a discussion on faith and culture, see 66-67; for a discussion on how Christian faith found connection with Greek philosophy, see 201-202; and for the basis of dialogue with other religions, see 75 and 169.

27. Ibid., 201-202.

28. Ibid., 174 - 175.

29. Ibid., 174.

30. Joseph Ratzinger, *Introduction to Christianity* (San Francisco: Ignatius, 1990), 20.

31. For a good summary of the Court of the Gentiles initiative see the article by Alessandra Nucci, "The Courtyard of the Gentiles," *The Catholic World Report* (May 13, 2011), http://www.catholicworldreport.com/Item/704/the_courtyard_of_the_gentiles.aspx (accessed November 14, 2017).

32. Tracey Rowland, *Catholic Theology* (London: T&T Clark, 2017), 154. See Rowland's explanation of the correlationist approach to culture. For an example of the application of such a method, see Kathryn Tanner, *Theories of Culture: A New Agenda for Theology* (Augsburg: Fortress Press, 1997).

33. Joseph Ratzinger, "Homily at the Cappella Papale Mass, 'Pro Eligendo Roman Pontifice,'" http://www.vatican.va/gpII/documents/homily-pro-eligendo-pontifice_20050418_en.html (accessed November 2, 2017).

34. Joseph Ratzinger, *Principles of Catholic Theology* (San Francisco: Ignatius, 1987), 393.

35. Joseph Ratzinger, "Homily at the Cappella Papale Mass, 'Pro Eligendo Roman Pontifice.'"

36. Joseph Ratzinger, *The Yes of Jesus Christ: Spiritual Exercises in Faith, Hope, and Love* (New York: Crossroad Publishing Company, 1991), 120.

37. Congregation for the Clergy, *The Gift of the Priestly Vocation*, 43.

38. See Francis, *Amoris Laetitia* (2016), sec. 300: "Discernment can never prescind from the Gospel demands as proposed by the Church." See the comment by Fr Matthew Schneider, "discernment should help find ways to live spousal fidelity and not ways to be excused from the Church's moral law," in Schneider "Amoris Laetitia Is about Accompaniment, not the Divorced and Remarried," *Crux, Taking the Catholic Pulse*, May 4, 2017, https://cruxnow.com/vatican/2017/05/04/amoris-laetitia-accompaniment-not-divorced-remarried/ (accessed, November 7, 2017). To back up this interpretation, Schneider refers to Jose Granados, Stephan Kampowski, and Juan Jose Perez-Soba, *Accompanying, Discerning, Integrating: A Handbook for the Pastoral Care of the Family According to Amoris Laetitia* (Steubenville, OH: Emmaus Road Publishing, 2017).

39. John Monroe, "How the Two Standards Meditation Can Help Outside of a Retreat," https://www.ignatianspirituality.com/ignatian-prayer/the-spiritual-exercises/how-the-two-standards-meditation-can-help-outside-of-a-retreat (accessed November 15, 2017).

40. Francis, "Clericalism Distances People from the Church," Vatican Radio, 13. 12. 2016, http://en.radiovaticana.va/news/2016/12/13/pope_clericalism_distances_the_people_from_the_church/1278688 (accessed August 23, 2017).

41. Hannah Brockhaus, "In Stressing Error of Clericalism, Francis Calls for Humble Priests," (Dec 13, 2016), http://www.catholicnewsagency.com/news/in-stressing-error-of-clericalism-francis-calls-for-humble-priests-32780/(accessed August 23, 2017).

42. Francis, "Presentation of the Christmas Greeting to the Roman Curia, Address of his Holiness Pope Francis, Clementine Hall," Monday, December 22, 2014, https://w2.vatican.va/content/francesco/en/speeches/2014/december/documents/papa-francesco_20141222_curia-romana.html (accessed August 23, 2017).

43. Ratzinger, *Christianity and the Crisis of Cultures*, 41.

44. Zygmunt Bauman, *Liquid Modernity* (Malden, MA: Blackwell, 2000), 82.

45. Peter Berger and Thomas Luckmann. *The Social Construction of Reality: A Treatise in the Sociology of Knowledge* (New York: Random House, 1966).

46. Ratzinger, *Introduction to Christianity*, 41.

47. John Paul II, *Pastores Dabo Vobis*, sec. 8.

48.   Hans Urs von Balthasar, *The Moment of Christian Witness* (San Francisco: Communio Books, Ignatius, 1994), 63.

49.   Ratzinger, "Homily of Joseph Ratzinger, Dean of the College of Cardinals for Mass of Papal Conclave, April 18, 2017," http://www.vatican.va/gpII/documents/homily-pro-eligendo-pontifice_20050418_en.html (accessed October 17, 2017).

50.   Ratzinger, *Introduction to Christianity*, sec. 40.

51.   Ratzinger, "The Biblical Foundations of Priesthood," 620.

52.   Ibid., 621.

53.   Ratzinger, *In the Beginning: A Catholic Understanding of Creation and the Fall* (London: T&T Clark, 1995), 38.

54.   See Paul VI, *Lumen Gentium* (1964), Chapter 1.

55.   Marc Ouellet, "Priestly Ministry at the Service of Ecclesial Communion," *Communio* 23 (Winter 1996): 683.

56.   Ibid.

57.   Romano Guardini, *The Reality of the Church* (Brescia, 1973) quoted in Joseph Ratzinger, "The Ecclesiology of Vatican II" in *Origins*, 15 (1985): 371.

58.   *Benedict XVI, Farewell address of Pope Benedict XVI to the Cardinals in Rome, Thursday, 28 February 2013*, https://w2.vatican.va/content/benedict-xvi/en/speeches/2013/february/documents/hf_ben-xvi_spe_20130228_congedo-cardinali.html. Italics mine (accessed September 4, 2017).

59.   See Joseph Ratzinger, *Daughter Sion: Meditations on the Church's Marian Belief* (San Francisco: Ignatius Press, 1983). See also Mary Frances Mc Kenna, *Innovation within Tradition: Joseph Ratzinger and Reading the Women of Scripture* (Augsburg: Fortress Press, 2015).

60.   See *Lumen Gentium*, sec. 62. "This maternity of Mary in the order of grace began with the consent which she gave in faith at the Annunciation and which she sustained without wavering beneath the cross, and lasts until the eternal fulfilment of all the elect," and John Paul II *Redemptoris Mater* (1987), sec. 6, 13-19.

61.   Joseph Ratzinger and Hans Urs von Balthasar, *Mary: The Church at the Source* (San Francisco: Ignatius Press, 1997), 110.

62.   G. J. McAleer, *Ecstatic Morality and Sexual Politics: A Catholic and Antitotalitarian Theory of the Body* (New York: Fordham University Press, 2005), 75, 79.

63.   Ibid., 83. Here McAleer quotes from St Thomas Aquinas, *III Sentences*, d. 27, q. 1, a.1. ad 4. "Love is ecstatic because what boils steams, boils over, and spills out of itself." See Aquinas, *Sentencia Libri De Anima*. Commentary on Aristotle's De Anima, trans. Kenelm Foster, O.P. and Sylvester Humphries, O.P. (New Haven: Yale University Press, 1951).

64.   According to St. Thomas Aquinas, *pathos* "means being affected by someone outside of oneself." See St. Thomas Aquinas's treatise on the passions. *ST* I-II, 22-48.

65. Prayer of St Elizabeth of the Trinity, "O My God, Trinity whom I adore." November 21, 1904, in *Elizabeth of the Trinity: The Complete Works, Volume One. General Introduction Major Spiritual Writings* (Washington: ICS Publications, 1984), 183.

66. McAleer, *Ecstatic Morality*, 88.

67. See also Donald Calloway, *The Virgin Mary and Theology of the Body* (Massachusetts: Marian Press, 2006).

68. *Lumen Gentium*, sec. 10.

69. Ibid.

70. Ratzinger, *Gesammelte Schriften: Volk und Haus Gottes in Augustin's Lehre von der Kirch, die Dissertation und weitere Studien zu Theologie Augustinus und zu der Kirchenväter* (Freiburg, Basel, Vienna: Herder, 2011), 290-291. Translation mine.

71. Benedict XVI, *Sacramentum Caritatis* (2007), sec. 85. He writes of the life of Saint Polycarp of Smyrna: "the entire drama is described as a liturgy, with the martyr himself becoming Eucharist," http://www.vatican.va/holy_father/benedict_xvi/apost_exhortations/documents/hf_ben-xvi_exh_20070222_sacramentum-caritatis_en.html (accessed April 3, 2012).

72. Ibid. St Ignatius "sees himself as 'God's wheat' and desires to become in martyrdom 'Christ's pure bread.'"

73. Ibid.

74. St Elizabeth of the Trinity, "Heaven in Faith: Tenth Day," August 1906, in *Elizabeth of the Trinity: The Complete Works, Volume One. General Introduction Major Spiritual Writings* (Washington: ICS Publications, 1984), 111 - 113. In paragraphs 41-44, she describes her vocation and the vocation of all in the Church as "the praise of God's glory" and here, she describes some of the qualities of this vocation, which is a constant adoration and the beginning of the life of heaven on earth.

75. John Paul II, *Theology of the Body* (Boston: Daughters of St Paul, 1997), 278 (General audience of April 14, 1982).

76. John Paul II, *Theology of the Body*, 282 (General audience of April 28, 1982).

77. In serving the Church, the Bride, ultimately the service of the priest will be directed in service of Christ Himself (*Pastores Dabo Vobis*, sec. 23, *The Gift of the Priestly Vocation*, sec. 39). See also *Pastores Dabo Vobis*, sec. 23 and 39. He is required to "be capable of loving people with a heart which is new, generous and pure with genuine self-detachment, with full, constant and faithful dedication and at the same time with a kind of 'divine jealousy' (cf. 2 Cor 11:2) and even with a kind of maternal tenderness."

78. Marc Ouellet, "Priestly Ministry at the Service of Ecclesial Communion," *Communio* 23 (Winter 1996): 680.

79. John Paul II, *Pastores Dabo Vobis*, sec. 12.

80.   Ratzinger, "Biblical Foundations of Priesthood," 626.

81.   Ibid., 627.

82.   Hans Urs von Balthasar, *The Moment of Christian Witness* (San Francisco: Ignatius Press, 1994), 149.

83.   St. John Vianney, quoted in B. Nodet, *Jean-Marie Vianney, Curé d' Ars: Sa Pensee, Son Couer* (Cerf: Broché, 2006) quoted in the *Catechism of the Catholic Church*, sec. 83.

"WHAT ARE YOU LOOKING AT?": SCREENS, FACES, AND THE PLACE OF CONTEMPLATION IN SEMINARY FORMATION

CHRISTOPHER RUDDY

St. Irenaeus famously wrote that "the glory of God is the living human person," but he immediately followed that statement with another one: "But the life of the human person is the vision of God." Christianity culminates in the beatific vision. A Benedictine bishop whom I know says that the Devil would much rather have us look at an electronic screen than at a Host. The Devil knows that we are contemplative animals; and so, he wants to pull our gaze away from reality to virtuality—and, it seems, no better means has ever been devised for distracting our gaze than electronic screens, particularly those on smartphones.

The stakes, then, are high—for what we look at determines who we are. I want, in this essay, first to examine the challenge of contemporary technology and its connection to the presence of acedia in seminarian and priestly life. Second, I will consider contemplation and leisure as antidotes to the distraction and acedia fostered by the abuse of technology. I will conclude by addressing the implications of the interplay between alienation-acedia and contemplation for seminary formation and priestly ministry.

Alienation and Acedia: "Partial Attention and Downturned Eyes"

A decade ago, the technology journalist Nicholas Carr wrote for the *Atlantic* an article, "Is Google Making Us Stupid?,"[1] which he later expanded into his 2010 book *The Shallows: What the Internet Is Doing to Our Brains*.[2] His central concern is "the permanent state of distractedness that defines the online life. . . . The distractions in our lives have been proliferating for a long time, but never has there been a medium that, like the Net, has been programmed to so widely scatter our attention and to do it so insistently."[3] Our brains are continually being rewired, for good and for ill; but the electronic screen does so in a way that fosters short-term, immediate stimulation and reward. Attention spans decline markedly; the concentration and patience needed for reading books and long articles atrophy. Such distractedness leaves us in what Carr calls "the shallows," an existence lacking in intellectual, emotional, and relational depth. He also notes that in "the shallows," we lose our empathy:

> It's not only deep thinking that requires a calm, attentive mind. It's also empathy and compassion. . . . [W]hile the human brain reacts very quickly to demonstrations of physical pain—when you see someone injured, the primitive pain centers in your own brain activate almost immediately—the more sophisticated mental process of empathizing with psychological suffering unfolds much more slowly.

[T]he more distracted we become, the less able we are to experience the subtlest, most distinctively human forms of empathy, compassion, and other emotions. . . . It would be rash to jump to the conclusion that the Internet is undermining our moral sense. It would not be rash to suggest that as the Net reroutes our vital paths and diminishes our capacity for contemplation, it is altering the depth of our emotions as well as our thoughts.[4]

Carr's insights have been confirmed in recent years by Sherry Turkle and Jean Twenge. Turkle, the Abby Rockefeller Mauzé Professor of the Social Studies of Science and Technology at the Massachusetts Institute of Technology, has written several books on technology and relationships, such as *Life on the Screen: Identity in the Age of the Internet* (1995) and *Alone Together: Why We Expect More from Technology and Less from Each Other* (2011). Her most recent book, *Reclaiming Conversation: The Power of Talk in a Digital Age*,[5] might seem like an odd choice for our consideration of contemplation, given its emphasis on speech, but she shares Carr's concern for technology's corrosive effects on interiority and relationships. Structuring her book around Henry David Thoreau's comment in *Walden* that he had "three chairs in my house; one for solitude, two for friendship, and three for society"—she argues that the "digital age" has dramatically affected—often for worse—all three sets of relationships; the desire for "distraction, comfort, and efficiency"[6] alienates us personally, relationally, and communally. She notes the striking reality that even the mere visible presence of a cellphone makes conversation shallower and less connective; she notes, with sad irony: *"Even a silent phone disconnects us."*[7]

Like Carr, Turkle laments the loss of empathy and connectedness generated by our technologies. We are losing the ability to focus and can no longer see faces: "What are we to make of the fact that when we have our phones out, our eyes are downward. . . . We've seen more and more research suggest that the always-on life erodes our capacity for empathy."[8] That decline in empathy—a drop of nearly 40 percent over the last twenty years, most of it in the last decade—is due to students having less direct face-to-face contact with each other.[9] "The development of empathy needs face-to-face conversation. And it needs eye contact."[10] Eye-contact develops the areas of the brain involved with attachment:

> [A]ll of these technologies of partial attention and downturned eyes . . . touch the most intimate moments in human development. They are poised to accompany children as they try to develop the capacity for attachment, solitude, and empathy. What looks like coping can take its toll.[11]

Turkle is more optimistic than I (and, perhaps, Carr) about our ability to control our use of technology—she wants us to "step up" with resilience to the challenge, and not "step back" in defeat[12]—but she makes some valuable suggestions near the end of *Reclaiming Conversation*: "*Remember the power of your phone. It's not just an accessory.*" "*Slow down.*" "*Protect your creativity. Take your time. Take quiet time.*" "*Think of unitasking as the next big thing.*"[13] This last bit of advice is essential in an increasingly fast-paced and distracted (and distracting) age: study after study proves that we are far less good at multitasking than we think we are. Craving the "quick hit of the new"[14] and trying to keep up with endless texts and e-mails, we are

losing our humanity by losing our capacity for sustained
attentiveness to ourselves, other people, and God: "Now we
are ready to reclaim our attention—for solitude, for friendship, for society."[15] She concludes her book thusly:

> This is our nick of time and our line to toe: to
> acknowledge the unintended consequences of
> technologies to which we are vulnerable, to respect the
> resilience that has always been ours. We have time to
> make the corrections. And to remember who we are—
> creatures of history, of deep psychology, of complex
> relationships. Of conversations artless, risky, and
> *face-to-face.*[16]

The challenges identified by Carr and Turkle will only
intensify in the years ahead. Jean Twenge, a psychologist
teaching at San Diego State University, has recently written
*iGen: Why Today's Super-Connected Kids Are Growing Up Less
Rebellious, More Tolerant, Less Happy—and Completely Unprepared
for Adulthood* (*and What That Means for the Rest of Us).*[17]
That verbose, commercial title aside, Twenge's book makes
a frightening, persuasive argument that the smartphone—
particularly as a platform for social media—has directly
contributed to massive, striking declines in the mental-social-
psychological health of what she calls "iGen"—those born
between 1995 and 2012, who have never known a world
without the Internet and, increasingly, smartphones. iGen
high school seniors from all types of backgrounds report
spending an average of six hours a day using new media: 2¼
hours texting, 2 hours on the Internet, 1½ on gaming, and ½
hour on video chat; virtually all of their leisure time is spent

in front of a screen, and daily face-to-face time with friends has declined significantly—especially since 2010.[18]

That increase in screen-time and decrease in face-time corresponds to a dramatic decline in iGen mental health vis-à-vis previous generations such as Generation X (born between 1965 and 1981) and the Millennials (roughly 1981 to 1995). Twenge is blunt: "[A]ll screen activities are linked to less happiness, and all nonscreen activities are linked to more happiness."[19] Furthermore, that decline rapidly accelerates around 2011-2012, precisely the time when smartphones—which were introduced in 2007—became widespread among children and teens.[20] The statistics are sobering: rates of unhappiness, loneliness, depression, and suicide have all increased, sometimes dramatically (e.g., depressive symptoms among 8th- to 12th-grade girls have skyrocketed from 22 percent in 2012 to nearly 34 percent in 2015—an increase of 50 percent in only three years).[21] As Twenge puts it, iGens are "both the physically safest generation and the most mentally fragile."[22] Although girls seem to be more adversely affected than boys, possibly due to bullying relationships on social media, I believe that it would be foolish to deny that seminary formation will be affected dramatically by such developments in the years to come.[23]

Carr, Turkle, and Twenge all point to a common, deep, and radical problem: the alienation and fragmentation generated by our (ab)use of technology. That alienation has roots, I suspect, in the nearly-forgotten sin of acedia. The Benedictine Jean-Charles Nault has made a powerful case that acedia is the besetting sin of our time.[24] Drawing upon ancient and medieval sources—especially Evagrius and Aquinas—he understands acedia as a sin that eludes simple definition; it can be characterized as "languor, torpor, despair, laziness, boredom, . . . disgust,"[25] and yet it goes beyond each of these conditions. For Evagrius, acedia could be understood as a "lack of spiritual energy"[26] that manifests itself temporally and spatially; above all, it shows itself in restlessness, both physical and spiritual.[27] For Aquinas, acedia is especially "sadness about spiritual good" and "disgust with activity."[28]

Acedia is particularly insidious because, although it is the "noonday demon" that strikes at the height of day, it "plunges the heart of the person that it afflicts into the gray fog of weariness and the night of despair."[29] It threatens to make us impervious to the Holy Spirit's forgiveness and consolation.[30] Deeply misunderstood and even forgotten, acedia is, nonetheless, "perhaps the root cause of the greatest crisis in the Church today."[31]

For the priest, acedia manifests itself especially in (1) discouragement in the face of ministerial exhaustion, frustration, and a seeming lack of success; (2) the rupturing of ecclesial communion through the choice of "my" ministry and a "bitter attitude toward authority"[32]; and (3) activism-hyperactivity and the destructive "compensations" that flow from a failure to pray:

> The priest no longer has time to pray, but paradoxically he happens to "waste time" in secondary or even plainly harmful activities. I am thinking, in particular, of the sensitive question of using the internet and social networks. Although the new means of communication are a valuable aid for practical ministry and personal formation and are obviously an organizational time-saver, we must not forget the dangers they pose for the spiritual life: the loss of time, superficial relationships, real dangers

to purity of heart and of the body, loss of freedom, and dulling of the conscience. How many priests admit having trouble managing their relationship with the internet, recognizing that they devote too much time to it, with the risk of making it an opportunity to compensate for the difficulties inherent in the performance of their daily ministry![33]

The main remedy to this priestly form of acedia, Nault writes, is a humility in which the priest accepts his inadequacy and lets the Holy Spirit "take possession of him more and more each day, and of his emotional and spiritual dynamics as well."[34] That holiness is both a Divine gift and the "fruit of his fidelity."[35] I am convinced that such holiness—and the healing of acedia's alienation and hyperactivity—comes about especially through contemplation and worship.

Contemplation, Leisure, and Worship

The development of a well-rounded mind requires both an ability to find and quickly parse a wide range of information and a capacity for open-ended reflection. There needs to be time for efficient data collection and time for inefficient contemplation, time to operate the machine and time to sit idly in the garden. We need to work in Google's "world of numbers," but we also need to able to retreat to Sleepy Hollow. The problem today is that we're losing our ability to strike a balance between those two very different states of mind. Mentally, we're in perpetual locomotion.[36]

These words of Nicholas Carr find an echo in what Dysmas de Lassus, the Prior of La Grande Chartreuse in France, calls "suffocation syndrome." De Lassus notes that

Carthusian candidates often find, in the silence of retreat, that "memories, desires, hurts, and fears" previously buried under the distraction of constant activity emerge and generate pain, which some then seek to suppress through a return to "permanent noise."[37] Seemingly safe, such noise—aural or visual—is, in reality, sick and suffocating.[38] Think, for instance, of the screens that are omnipresent in airports, eateries, and even on gas pumps.

Carr's "perpetual locomotion" and de Lassus's "permanent noise" both point to the snowballing presence of acedia in the age of smartphones. Oscillating between lethargy and hyperactivity, acedia is the sin of our time. All of this can seem like bad news, and it clearly is; but, perhaps, it may also indicate that the time is ripe for what Father Donald Haggerty has called a "contemplative revolution" marked by "the fundamental importance of silent prayer in hours alone before the gaze of God."[39] Such prayer, marked by an interplay of blindness and vision, fosters sustained consideration of, and vulnerability to, others. Haggerty's words second Carr's earlier comments on the relationship between attentiveness and empathy (and, conversely, distractedness and indifference):

> A narrow and impure vision accompanies all habits of spiritual inattention. When we are distracted and unfocused in our mind, we are easily blind to the realities immediately before our eyes. . . . Our days can become an ensemble of hasty, fitful glances rather than a discipline of purposeful and watchful attention. The result is that receptivity to the spiritual reality of other persons diminishes. We perceive little of the actual suffering in a lonely person's face or the features of a person of strong

spiritual character. . . . Yet cultivating an openness to being moved and wounded when we look at other faces is precisely the humanity to which we must courageously aspire if we are to see as God made our eyes to see.[40]

Contemplation, thus, helps us to receive the gaze of God and to see Him and other people better. Far from pulling us away from reality and locking us up in ourselves, it leads us to reality and to relationship. It is an essential remedy to the alienation and distraction, the torpor and hyperactivity of acedia.

Prayer, moreover, reminds us that God is in charge, not we.[41] When we begin to trust God's initiative, the result is not sloth but life. The late American Jesuit Thomas Green likened mature prayer—that is, prayer that has undergone the dark night of the spirit—to floating, in contrast to swimming and to drifting.[42] Where the "swimmer" seeks to control his or her movement toward God, and the "drifter" sinks through a lazy response to Divine currents and waves, the "floater" trustingly surrenders; he or she is active yet relaxed, trusting that the "tide" of God's loving providence will carry one to God much more surely than drifting or even swimming. The parallel to acedia is evident: swimming is hyperactivity; drifting is listlessness. Each is one side of the same coin of a refusal to surrender and, thereby, fully unite one's will to God's.

Such a contemplative life and vision are fostered by what Josef Pieper has called the bond between leisure and worship. He notes that, in a modern world marked by a cult of "total labor,"[43] whether communist or capitalist, leisure is commonly seen as laziness, idleness, sloth, distraction, or—at best—resting so as to work more productively. The irony is that such a modern worldview identifies as leisure precisely what the ancients and medievals viewed as acedia: slackness and workaholism. In such a worldview, Aquinas's understanding of acedia as a sin against the Third Commandment is nearly incomprehensible.[44]

The true opposite of acedia, however, is not industriousness, but affirmation: of self, of creation, of God. Genuine leisure is rooted in silence, receptivity, openness, serenity, "looseness," (think of the parallel to Thomas Green's contemplative "floater").[45] Most deeply, it is an assent to reality, a "happy and cheerful affirmation of [one's] own being, [one's] acquiescence in the world and in God—which is to say love."[46] It is, in Pieper's fine phrase, "a receptive attitude, a contemplative attitude, and it is not only the occasion but also the capacity for steeping oneself in the whole of creation."[47] Leisure, thus, depends upon a contemplative vision that sees reality as it truly is. Leisure is, ironically, more realistic than an illusory, hard-nosed utilitarianism.

Leisure, in turn, is rooted in Divine worship. Such festivity is grounded in affirmation of what is, in the orders of both creation and redemption.[48] In terms of creation, there is possible no more radical human assent to the world than praise of its creator,[49] who Himself assents to His handiwork as "very good." Sunday, in the first instance, celebrates "the gift of being created."[50] Still more expansively, Christian liturgy is:

> "unbounded Yea- and Amen-saying." Every prayer closes with the word: Amen, thus it is good, thus shall it be, *ainsi soit-il.* What is the *Alleluia* but a cry of jubilation? The heavenly adoration in the Apocalyptic vision is

also a single great acclamation, composed of reiterated exclamations of Hail, Praise, Glory, Thanks. . . . Christian worship sees itself as an act of affirmation that expresses itself in praise, glorification, thanksgiving for the whole of reality and existence.[51]

Pieper sums up this "leisurely," festive worldview in his claim that "No more rightful, more comprehensive and fundamental an affirmation [of all existence] can be conceived" than Easter, the Eighth Day that recapitulates and transforms the seven days of creation and rest.[52]

Pieper's largely philosophical analysis finds theological confirmation in what I would call a doxological ecclesiology. Ecclesially, acedia manifests itself not only in tepidity and managed decline, but in what I call the "danger of a busy Church,"[53] an activism that can mask the underlying despair and listlessness of acedia. Rowan Williams has said that, absent sustained contemplative practices, the Church will "run the risk of trying to sustain faith on the basis of an untransformed set of human habits—with the all-too-familiar result that the church comes to look unhappily like so many purely human institutions, anxious, busy, competitive, and controlling."[54]

By contrast, *Lumen Gentium's* much-neglected seventh chapter—"The Eschatological Character of the Pilgrim Church and Its Union with the Heavenly Church"—strikingly affirms that the Church's "deepest" or most "intimate" (*intimae*) vocation is twofold: mutual love and the "praise of the most holy Trinity."[55] The Church is most truly itself, on earth as in heaven, when it lovingly worships its Lord. Worship is not simply a means, but an end—*the* end—in itself.[56]

In this precise sense, orthodoxy (right praise) is the anti-dote to acedia. We can praise rightly when, as Pieper reminds us, we see rightly the gifts of nature and supernature. We are made whole in looking into the face of an icon, not at the screen of an idol. Priests, who are configured to act in the person of Christ the Head and Shepherd of the Church, have a special responsibility in this regard. And it is of paramount importance that seminarians be formed in such a contempla-tive, doxological manner, lest they succumb to the discourage-ment and activist burnout that Nault identifies as particularly priestly temptations. They will not otherwise be able to over-come in themselves or in their people the sin of acedia.

Implications

Objections can easily be raised to the vision that I have sketched so far: it is impractical, irresponsible, otherworldly, even dangerous; it contributes to laziness and self-indulgence, to a kind of narcissism and self-referentiality that is deadly to mission and ministry; seminary formation should be about forming pastors, not monks. Donald Haggerty grasps the heart of these criticisms: "This choice for what can seem to some extent a solitary path to God may give the appearance of a withdrawal from the primary importance of evangeli-cal witness in the Church, which remains always a perennial need."[57] There is the further complication that, save for most Carthusians, few people—let alone diocesan seminarians and priests—can abstain entirely from the use of technology and screens. The recovering alcoholic at least has the possibility (and necessity) of complete abstinence from alcohol, but the screen addict (or even daily user) can rarely practice such abstinence. So, how do we go forward in an environment

of alienation and distraction, an environment that, as Jean
Twenge argues, is getting worse in terms of mental health?

Most broadly, Haggerty is right in rejecting the facile
opposition of contemplation and action, of prayerfulness
and engagement:

> Those . . . who think that prayer impedes a life of active
> generosity or is simply incompatible with a busy life in the
> world are mistaken. . . . [E]veryone who is serious about
> the pursuit of prayer seems always to possess a more
> intense spiritual energy for the active demands of life.
> The saints are a vivid testimony of this truth.[58]

I suspect, too, that much reticence or even resistance in
the face of prayer stems not only from (ultimately misguided)
concerns about pastoral effectiveness, but also the lurking
sense that prayer can be hard, dry, unrewarding, and painful;
calls to be more prayerful can reveal our selfishness and sloth,
our unwillingness to change in response to God's presence in
our lives. One thinks again of Aquinas's definition of acedia
as "sadness about spiritual good" and "disgust with activity."

Specifically, apart from quite practical guidelines such as
the avoidance—except in rare circumstances—of iBreviary
and similar apps, or Andy Crouch's "Ten Tech-Wise Com-
mitments"[59] (e.g., number 4: "We wake up before our devices
do, and they 'go to bed' before we do."), I suggest four areas
that can contribute to a more fruitful seminary formation
in a time of distraction, alienation, and waning faith: nature,
pedagogy, horarium, and faces.

Nature

Nicholas Carr notes that scientific studies stretching over two decades have shown that time spent in "quiet rural settings" fosters "greater attentiveness, stronger memory, and generally improved cognition."[60] He mentions a recent study in which a test group, after having taken a series of tests involving memory and attentiveness, was split in half, with one group spending an hour walking through woods and the other spending an hour walking in a downtown city. Both groups were re-tested at the conclusion of the hour, and the "nature-walkers" markedly outpaced the "city-walkers"; amazingly, exposure to even photographs of nature (as opposed to those of cities) improves cognition and attentiveness.[61] Carr notes that "there is no Sleepy Hollow on the Internet, no peaceful spot where contemplativeness can work its restorative magic. There is only the endless, mesmerizing buzz of the urban street." The goal, he writes, is not to give up the "invigorating, inspiring" stimulation of the Internet, but to recognize and resist the exhaustion and distraction that it generates.[62] I remember, too, Louis Dupré teaching an undergraduate course on mystical experience and almost off-handedly telling his students that academic types need to work with their hands, that they should have "soil in their hands and under their fingernails." It would be good to foster in seminarians the habit of taking a daily walk, in nature wherever possible, even if only for fifteen minutes.

Pedagogy

Students, especially iGens, are reading much less than in decades past. Jean Twenge notes that the percentage of teens who read a book or magazine "nearly every day" has fallen from roughly 60 percent in the late 1970s to 16 percent in 2015.[63] She proposes that teachers and publishers reach today's students by "turning to e-textbooks with videos, interactive figures, and built-in quizzes—excellent ways to reach iGen."[64] Such approaches, she concludes with more than a whiff of desperation (or willful blindness), will perhaps lead "iGen—and the rest of us—[to] return to reading."[65]

The nature of online reading, however, contributes to a situation where, in Nicholas Carr's words, "The strip-mining of 'relevant content' replaces the slow excavation of meaning."[66] How can such "strip-mining" contribute to fostering intellectual and affective intimacy with God, that "resting on the heart of Christ" that James Keating has rightly identified as the spring of seminary theology?[67] How can we use a highly-addictive technology without succumbing to it? Technology cannot be completely rejected, but it does need to be countered. *Lectio divina* strikes me as an essential practice in our virtual age; it is a discipline in which linear, "academic" reading can be complemented and, where necessary, corrected by "spiral," ruminative, "spiritual" reading.[68] Additionally, I have generally prohibited the use of screens in the classroom and begin classes with a moment of silent prayer, concluded by the "Glory Be." I have tried to create a space, however imperfect, of interiority and reflection. Numerous students have expressed in course evaluations their appreciation for such practices.

Horarium

Having taught seminarians for nearly a decade, I continue to be struck by the differing, even competing, goals of seminary formation and education: the demands of human, intellectual, pastoral, and spiritual formation can clash with each other. Seminarians' busy schedules are sometimes justified in light of the demands of their future priestly ministry (which will only increase in the light of the continuing decline in the number of priests in full-time ministry), but what are the dangers of such busyness? James Keating has recently suggested, provocatively but calmly, that perhaps seminary curricula and degree programs be changed, to move from a Masters Degree in Divinity to a Masters Degree in the Arts, in order to make possible a deeper integration of study, prayer, and ministry in the life of the seminarian.[69] Such a proposal would likely dismay and even horrify many faculty involved with seminary formation; it raises the specter of amateurism and a lack of professionalism, of intellectual laziness, of a general lack of seriousness, and so on.

My predecessor at Catholic University offered one primary (and helpful) bit of advice when I began teaching seminarians: "Don't be afraid to make them work!" That need for hard work, however, actually comports well with Keating's call for seminarians to be true agents of their own formation.[70] Keating's proposal also resonates with Robert Barron's suggestion that priests see themselves—and be able to be seen by others—primarily as "mystery-bearers" and "soul-doctors."[71] Seminarians must be theologically well-formed if they are to meet the challenges of belief in our "secular age," where God seems literally incredible and irrelevant. But that intellectual formation must be shaped by its *telos*: the development of good, holy priests who can lead others to know and love and serve God. An often well-intentioned drive for "professionalism" can get in the way of that goal, and we need creativity to re-vision seminary formation.

Faces

Finally, but most importantly, the theme of beholding God's face is the heart of the matter.[72] Robert Wilken claims of Psalm 105:4—"Seek his face always," according to the Vulgate—that "More than any other passage in the Bible, it captures the spirit of early Christian thinking."[73] Our lives are meant to culminate in the beatific vision, of course. And yet, commending the search for God's face may seem like supporting mom and apple pie: who could be against it? The challenge, however, is to make that "face-seeking" concrete and regular. We must look *down* at screens less, as Sherry Turkle notes,[74] and more *across* to Christ in the tabernacle and the monstrance, to Christ in the neighbor. We need more "face time" and less "FaceTime"! Screens, in their unceasing stimulation, foster the instability, hyperactivity, and distractedness so characteristic of acedia; we are everywhere and nowhere at once. Only attentiveness to faces—and not screens—can heal and save us.

On the natural level, Turkle and Twengle, we have seen, establish the clear correlation between face-to-face contact and good mental health. On a supernatural level, Eucharistic adoration must be a daily, substantial part of every seminarian's and priest's life; a half hour in silence would seem to be a minimum, preferably an hour. We need to look at Jesus, and we need to let ourselves be seen by Him, to realize that He desires to gaze at each one of us and that He delights in us. The famous comment on Eucharistic adoration by St. John Vianney's parishioner never grows old: "I look at Him, and He looks at me."

Furthermore, as *Pastores Dabo Vobis* notes, the encounter with the person of Christ leads necessarily to "seeking Christ in people":

> The spiritual life is, indeed, an interior life, a life of intimacy with God, a life of prayer and contemplation. But this very meeting with God, and with his fatherly love for everyone, brings us face to face with the need to meet our neighbor, to give ourselves to others, to serve in a humble and disinterested fashion, following the example which Jesus proposed to everyone as a program of life when he washed the feet of the apostles: "I have given you an example, that you also should do as I have done to you" (John 13:15).[75]

In this way, love of God and love of neighbor, gazing at the face of Christ in Himself and in others, flow together and fructify each other: "And we all, with unveiled face, beholding the glory of the Lord, are being changed into his likeness from one degree of glory to another" (2 Cor 3:18). In sum, we become what—or, rather, whom—we look at. Will it be the screen or the face of Christ, for those in clerical formation?

NOTES

1. Nicholas Carr, "Is Google Making Us Stupid?," *The Atlantic*: https://www.theatlantic.com/magazine/archive/2008/07/is-google-making-us-stupid/306868/.

2. Nicholas G. Carr, *The Shallows: What the Internet is Doing to Our Brains* (New York: W. W. Norton & Company, 2010).

3. Ibid., 112-113.

4. Ibid., 220-221.

5. Sherry Turkle, *Reclaiming Conversation: The Power of Talk in a Digital Age* (New York: Penguin Press, 2015).

6. Ibid., 9.

7. Ibid., 21. Emphasis in original.

8. Ibid., 171.

9. Ibid., 21, 171. See also 324-25: "There is nothing wrong with texting or email or videoconferencing. And there is everything right with making them technically better, more intuitive, easier to use. But no matter how good they get, they have an intrinsic limitation: People require eye contact for emotional stability and social fluency. A lack of eye contact is associated with depression, isolation, and the development of antisocial traits such as exhibiting callousness. And the more we develop these psychological problems, the more we shy away from eye contact. Our slogan can be: If a tool gets in the way of our looking at each other, we should use it only when necessary. It shouldn't be the first thing we turn to."

10. Turkle, *Reclaiming Conversation*, 170.

11. Ibid., 171.

12. Ibid., 14.

13. See Turkle, *Reclaiming Conversation*, 319-30. Emphasis in original.

14. Turkle, *Reclaiming Conversation*, 321.

15. Ibid., 361.

16. Ibid., 362. Emphasis added.

17. Jean Twenge, *iGen: Why Today's Super-Connected Kids Are Growing Up Less Rebellious, More Tolerant, Less Happy—and Completely Unprepared for Adulthood* (*and What That Means for the Rest of Us* (New York: Atria Books, 2017).

18. Ibid., 51, 71-72.

19. Ibid., 77-78. Twenge identifies five "no-screen" activities that correspond to higher levels of happiness: "In-person social interaction," "Sports/exercise," "Religious services," "Print media," and "Working." Would it be too much to see here the simple, deep wisdom of cenobitic monasticism: a communal life centered on prayer, *lectio divina*, and work?

20. Ibid., 4.

21. Ibid., 93-118.

22. Ibid., 312.

23. Twenge is good at description, weaker at analysis. She particularly lacks any sense of the purpose of life, of teleology and a vision of human flourishing. Thus, she is able to describe the symptoms, but cannot really identify either the disease or the cure, so to speak.

24. Jean-Charles Nault, *The Noonday Devil: Acedia, The Unnamed Evil of Our Times*, trans. Michael J. Miller (San Francisco: Ignatius, 2015).

25. Ibid., 26.

26. Ibid., 28.

27. See Gabriel Bunge's *Despondency: The Spiritual Teaching of Evagrius Ponticus on Acedia* (Yonkers, NY: St. Vladimir's Seminary Press, 2012), esp. 67-69, 92-93.

28. Nault, *The Noonday Devil*, 57-58.

29. Ibid., 20.

30. Nault notes, in this context, that the last "instrument of good work" commended by the *Rule of St. Benedict* is "never to despair of God's mercy" (RB 4, 72). Nault continues, "Of all these instruments of the spiritual art that Benedict recommends, he concludes with the one that must not be abandoned in any circumstances. If it were necessary to keep only one, he seems to tell us, let it be that one!" (*The Noonday Devil*, 83).

31. Ibid., 18.

32. Ibid., 176.

33. Ibid., 174-175.

34. Ibid., 177.

35. Ibid., 177.

36. Carr, *The Shallows*, 168.

37. Robert Cardinal Sarah with Nicolas Diat, *The Power of Silence: Against the Dictatorship of Noise*, trans. Michael J. Miller (San Francisco: Ignatius, 2017), 228.

38. Analogously, Josef Pieper says, "the average person of our time loses the ability to see because *there is too much to see*" (emphasis in original), in *Only the Lover Sings: Art and Contemplation*, trans. Lothar Krauth (San Francisco: Ignatius, 1990), 32.

39. Donald Haggerty, *The Contemplative Hunger* (San Francisco: Ignatius, 2016), 22.

40. Ibid., 76-77. See Carr, *The Shallows*, 220-21.

41. More than, perhaps, anyone in the contemporary Church, the English Carmelite Ruth Burrows has emphasized that prayer is primarily God's work; it is not "*our* activity, *our* getting in touch with God, *our* coming to grips with or making ourselves desirable to God. We can do none of these things, nor do we need to, for God is there ready to do everything for us, loving us unconditionally. . . . Never does the initiative lie with us. We haven't to persuade God to be good to us but have only to

surrender to the goodness that surrounds us." (*Essence of Prayer* [Mahwah, NJ: HiddenSpring, 2006/2012], 28, 37.)

42. See Thomas H. Green, *When the Well Runs Dry: Prayer Beyond the Beginnings* (Notre Dame, IN: Ave Maria, 2007), esp. 156-62, 178, 183-90.

43. Josef Pieper, *Leisure: The Basis of Culture*, trans. Alexander Dru (San Francisco: Ignatius, 2009), 20. In this view, the human person "seems to mistrust everything that is effortless; he can only enjoy, with a good conscience, what he has acquired with toil and trouble; he refuses to have anything as a gift." (35-36).

44. Pieper, *Leisure*, 45.

45. Ibid., 47: "Leisure is not the attitude of mind of those who actively intervene, but of those who are open to everything; not of those who grab and grab hold, but of those who leave the reins loose and who are free and easy themselves."

46. Ibid., 45.

47. Ibid., 46-47.

48. See St. John Paul II's 1998 apostolic letter *Dies Domini*, whose first chapter reflects on creation and whose second chapter speaks of salvation.

49. Josef Pieper, *In Tune with the World: A Theory of Festivity*, trans. Richard and Clara Winston (South Bend, IN: St. Augustine's Press, 1999), 31.

50. Ibid., 47-48. Pieper cites here the *Summa Theologiae* I-II, Q. 100, Art. 5, ad 2. He says elsewhere: "I really do not know how an incorruptible mind, faced with the evil in the world, could keep from utter despair were it not for the logically tenable conviction that there is a divinely guaranteed Goodness of being which no amount of mischief can undermine. But that is the point of view of the man who sees the world as *creatura*—not to speak of the believer who is a confident of a salvation that infinitely surpasses all creaturely goodness" (*In Tune with the World*, 82).

51. Pieper, *In Tune with the World*, 37-38.

52. Ibid., 49. St. John Paul II's *Dies Domini* bears strong affinities with Pieper's thought on worship, festivity, and leisure, as well as on the relationship of these to the orders of creation and redemption.

53. See Christopher Ruddy, "'In My End Is My Beginning': *Lumen Gentium* and the Priority of Doxology," *Irish Theological Quarterly* 79 (2014): 144-64, at 162-63.

54. Rowan Williams, "Archbishop of Canterbury Addresses World Synod of Bishops," *Origins* 42 (October 25, 2012): 330-33, at 333.

55. Paul VI, *Lumen Gentium* (1964), sec. 51.

56. Pieper warns, "Leisure cannot be achieved at all when it is sought as a means to an end, even though that end be 'the salvation of Western civilization.' Celebration of God in worship cannot be done unless it is done for its own sake. That most sublime form of affirmation of the world as a whole is the fountainhead of leisure" (Pieper, *Leisure*, 72).

57.   Haggerty, *The Contemplative Hunger*, 23.

58.   Ibid., 18.

59.   See Andy Crouch, *The Tech-Wise Family: Everyday Steps for Putting Technology in Its Proper Place* (Grand Rapids, MI: BakerBooks, 2017).

60.   Carr, *The Shallows*, 219.

61.   Ibid., 219-20.

62.   Ibid., 220.

63.   Twenge, *iGen*, 60.

64.   Ibid., 307-08.

65.   Ibid., 65.

66.   Carr, *The Shallows*, 166. Reading comprehension and retention also decline markedly in online reading.

67.   James Keating, *Resting on the Heart of Christ: The Vocation and Spirituality of the Seminary Theologian* (Omaha, NE: IPF Publications, 2009).

68.   See James Keating, *Resting on the Heart of Christ: The Vocation and Spirituality of the Seminary Theologian* (Omaha, NE: IPF Publications, 2009), especially Chapter Three, "Study: Lectio and Research," and "Appendix: A Seminarian's Lectio: Reading to Know and to Receive Divine Love"; also, Perry Cahall, "Lecture Divina: The Fathers of the Church and Theological Pedagogy," in *Seminary Theology: Teaching in a Contemplative Way*, ed. James Keating (Omaha, NE: IPF Publications, 2010), 69-94.

69.   See James Keating, "Beyond Schooling: Seminaries, Integral Formation, and the Role of Academics," *Seminary Journal* 14.3 (Winter 2018).

70.   See James Keating, "The Seminary and Western Culture: Relationships that Promote Recovery and Holiness," *Nova et Vetera*, English Edition 14 (2016): 1099-1111, at 1107: "Such love and truth must be actively received by the man himself, since it is acknowledged that the structure and content of seminary alone are not sufficient to heal someone. A man cannot become holy if he passively exists within the set of relationships that is seminary."

71.   Robert Barron, "Priest as Bearer of the Mystery" and "Priest as Doctor of the Soul," in *Bridging the Great Divide: Musings of a Post-Liberal, Post-Conservative Evangelical Catholic* (Lanham, MD: Rowman and Littlefield, 2004). For instance, "To put it simply, the priest must be an authentically religious leader for his people; he must be, in the richest sense possible, spiritual director, mystical guide, shaman. I think that one of the greatest of the postconciliar mistakes was to turn the priest into psychologist, sociologist, social worker, counselor—anything but a uniquely religious leader. The authentic task of the mystagogue, as I've outlined it, is incomparably rich, constantly challenging; it is the career of the prophet, poet, and visionary. Why should we want to abandon such a role for that of second-rate psychologist or amateur social worker?

Now, someone might object that I am proposing a view of the priesthood that is elitist, intellectualistic, perhaps rather monkish. One might argue that all this literary and artistic refinement is fine for the seminary or university professor, but that it is unrealistic for the parish priest. In my view, nothing could be further from the truth. It is precisely the parish priest who has most contact with, and influence upon, the people of God, and it is therefore precisely the parish priest who should be best equipped to know, mediate, and express the Mystery. Sophistication of mind, heart, and sensibility is not a luxury for the parish priest; rather, it belongs to the very essence of who he is and what he does" (230-31).

72.   See two wise books on the theological significance of faces from David F. Ford: *The Shape of Living: Spiritual Directions for Everyday Life* (Grand Rapids, MI: Baker, 1997) and *Self and Salvation: Being Transformed* (New York: Cambridge, 1999).

73.   Robert Louis Wilken, *The Spirit of Early Christian Thought: Seeking the Face of God* (New Haven, CT: Yale, 2003), xxii.

74.   Turkle, *Reclaiming Conversation*, 171.

75.   John Paul II, *Pastores Dabo Vobis* (1992), sec. 49. Donald Haggerty's writings make a similar point about the Christian life *tout court* in their repeated insistence on the reciprocity of contemplation and service, especially to the poor. That reciprocity, he insists, is rooted in unceasing, unreserved self-offering.

Contemplation: Seeing His Face, Hearing His Voice

Janet E. Smith

"Oh, that today you would hear his voice: Do not harden your hearts"

(Psalm 95: 7-8)

The assignment to address the necessity of contemplation for seminarians is one that drives us to the very heart of the Christian: it is a deeply seated desire of those who love the Lord to see His face and to hear His voice. We want to see His face because He is love itself; and as we gaze on His face, we know we will be enraptured with His unsurpassable beauty and awash in His all-encompassing love. We expect to be captivated and riveted. We want to hear His voice because we want to be guided and consoled, and more importantly, to be in intimate conversation with Him.

A time-tested practice for getting a glimpse of God's face is the practice of contemplation. The term "contemplation" means to gaze intensely at something; and by gazing intently at the things God has made, we can often see God there— but it is in a mirror, dimly. Contemplative prayer is technically a very advanced level of prayer, and it is a level that I hope seminarians will reach relatively early in their practice of contemplation; but here, my references to contemplation are more general—they are to the receptive attentiveness to the Divine.[1]

There are many spiritual classics that speak to the value of contemplation. Two of the more recent valuable works on the subject that make classics more accessible are Fr. Thomas Dubay's *Fire Within: St Theresa of Avila, St John of the Cross, and the Gospel on Prayer* and Ralph Martin's *The Fulfillment of All Desire: A Guidebook for the Journey to God Based on the Wisdom of the Saints*.[2] Two fresh-off-the-press works promise to be of enduring assistance: Robert Cardinal Sarah's *The Power of Silence: Against the Dictatorship of Noise*[3] and the anonymously authored *In Sinu Jesu: When Heart Speaks to Heart—The Journal of a Priest at Prayer*[4] that records locutions received by a priest during adoration.

Silence is difficult, but it enables man to let himself be led by God. From silence is born silence. Through God the silent, we can attain silence. And man is unceasingly surprised by the light that pours forth then.[5]

Cultivating silence is very much a part of contemplation. Contemplation cannot be achieved without silence, and the practice of contemplation leads one to value silence all the more. Since Sarah's book is about the importance of silence, in addition to Scripture, I will be drawing upon his insights. Indeed, I find that there are many passages in his text where the word "silence" could be replaced with "contemplation" and the meaning would remain the same. Silence assists us both in seeing and in hearing! Among Sarah's initial reflections on silence are these:

At the heart of man there is an innate silence, for God abides in the innermost part of every person. God is silence, and this divine silence dwells in man. In God we are inseparably bound up with silence. The Church can affirm that mankind is the daughter of a silent God; for men are the sons of silence.

God carries us, and we live with him at every moment by keeping silence. Nothing will make us discover God better than his silence inscribed in the center of our being. If we do not cultivate this silence, how can we find God?[6]

It is possible to "know God" in some remote way without silence or contemplation, but those who crave an intimate relationship with the Trinity must cultivate the habit of contemplation and keeping a receptive silence.

"At present we see indistinctly, as in a mirror, but then face to face. At present I know partially; then I shall know fully, as I am fully known" (1 Cor 13:12).

We are graced to receive glimpses of God's love in this world. Some of the glimpses are extraordinary experiences, such as those had by mystics who are "taken up" to the next world and have ineffable experiences of beauty, truth, goodness, and unity. But since God's beauty, truth, goodness, and unity are everywhere, those who have acquired a habit of looking for and being responsive to these values have not infrequent occurrences of being swept off their feet by the mirrors of God's "face," whether stunned by some spectacular grand natural beauty of mountains, oceans, plains, skies, lakes, streams, and valleys; or a beautiful man, woman, or child; or a song or musical composition, painting, statue, or artifact that captures something of transcendent beauty. The grace and power of athletes can also be a source of awareness of what glories are possible. We can be stunned by truthfulness of an insight into reality or enchanted by some huge or small gesture of goodness; we rejoice in peaceful, harmonious unity with others. There is no shortage of possible encounters with glimpses of the Divine. They were designed to whet our appetites for the eternal possession of these and greater goods, and so they do.

I am certain that God gives to each believer a heart capable of hearing the language of creation. According to the expression of Ben Sirach the Sage, the Father has "set his eye on [men's] hearts" (Sir 17:8, Douay-Rheims), so that the believer may look at God, his neighbor, and the whole of creation with God's eyes.[7]

Seminarians must be encouraged to spend time in nature, hiking, fishing, kayaking, camping, or going to art museums or concerts that feature music that moves them to experience the transcendent. They must come to yearn to be in the presence of beauty, of a beauty that moves them to adore the author of all beauty. It would be best that they participate solo in such activities or at least to strive to have some time in solitude with natural or man-made, God-inspired beauty so they can let that beauty speak to their hearts. Even in the course of activities that are not intrinsically contemplative, they must be encouraged to cultivate a love for silence. They should, for instance, learn to love the quiet of driving in the car without the radio on.

The Liturgy, of course, should be the place where people can most reliably encounter the transcendent; but unfortunately, most liturgical styles of our times, at best, plunge people into experiencing a fairly small range of emotions—often of the maudlin sort. Yet, church remains a place where God can be reliably encountered because of the "Real Presence." Even those who are not Catholic, who have no knowledge or little understanding of the doctrine of the "Real Presence," often sense a presence of the Divine when in a space that houses a tabernacle. For those who believe in the "Real Presence," being in a space wherein the Blessed Sacrament is exposed can evoke powerful responses that range from wanting to throw one's whole body to the ground in a gesture of profound reverence—to desiring to run to the monstrance and give it a huge kiss, as one would when greeting one's dearest friend.

The practice of contemplation, especially in the presence of the exposed Eucharist in adoration, is precisely the kind of contemplation that Christians should crave and practice. Certainly, it should be a regular part of every seminarian's formation and then on-going practice in his priesthood; his appetite for such should whet the appetite of the flock he shepherds.

"For I am jealous of you with the jealousy of God, since I betrothed you to one husband to present you as a chaste virgin to Christ" (2 Cor 11:2).

The reality is this: we belong to Christ. We are His. All of us. All of us, female and male, are His spouses. As St. John Paul II taught, echoing the mystics, all souls are feminine in respect to God:

> From a linguistic viewpoint we can say that the analogy of spousal love found in the Letter to the Ephesians links what is "masculine" to what is "feminine," since, as members of the Church, men too are included in the concept of "bride." This should not surprise us, for Saint

> Paul, in order to express his mission in Jesus and in the
> Church, speaks of the "little children with whom he is
> again in travail" (cf. *Gal* 4:19). In the sphere of what is
> "human"—of what is humanly personal—"masculinity"
> and "femininity" are distinct, yet at the same time they
> complete and explain each other. This is also present
> in the great analogy of the "Bride" in the Letter to the
> Ephesians. In the Church every human being—male and
> female—is the "Bride," in that he or she accepts the gift
> of the love of Jesus the Redeemer, and seeks to respond
> to it with the gift of his or her own person. (*Mulieris
> Dignitatem*, 25)

God wants to possess our hearts as a bridegroom wants to
possess his bride.

The reality is also this: few males like to think of themselves as feminine. The seminarians I teach much prefer the
image of being a shepherd to that of being a bride. Scripture
has remedies for this discomfort. Certainly, God speaks quite
directly to men, leaders such as Moses, and prophets, such as
Elijah, to whom He gives very explicit marching orders, and
males generally like explicit marching orders. But the relationship of the soul to God is not one of soldier to general but
of beloved to lover. One of the most intimate portraits in
Scripture is the young Apostle John leaning against Jesus'
heart, and that image is tremendously attractive to seminarians; they want to be His intimate, beloved, chosen one. They
need to learn that contemplation is the way to connect their
hearts with Jesus' heart.

It is especially the consecrated who must intentionally live
out the quest to live in intimacy with Christ. It is especially
the consecrated who must respond generously to Christ's

desire to unite with His beloved. That means spending a lot of time in contemplation. It means wanting to learn to clear one's system of all thoughts, anxieties, hopes, and anything that might interfere with hearing's the Divine Spouse's/intimate friend's voice.

We can remain silent in the midst of the biggest messes and most despicable commotion, in the midst of the racket and howling of those infernal machines that draw us into the functionalism and activism by snatching us away from any transcendent dimension and from any interior life.[8]

There is hardly any need to establish that our age is one in which it is phenomenally difficult to find silence and in which there is little encouragement to foster an interior life. Sarah teaches that the practice of keeping silence, of contemplation, shapes our interior in such a way that we can access that silence, even in the midst of the noisiness and busyness of our lives.

"Through Sacred Scripture, when it is listened to and meditated upon in silence, divine graces are poured out on man. . . . Actually it is through long hours of poring over Sacred Scripture, after resisting all the attacks of the Prince of this world, that we will reach God."[9]

Learning how to pray is a lifetime task, much like it is a lifetime task for spouses to learn how to hear what the other is saying. Lovers "study" each other to learn how to respond rightly to them. Christians must study Jesus—we must learn who He is, what His ways are, and how He signals to us what He wants from us. Christians must become intimately familiar with Scripture for Scripture is the record we have of what Jesus said and did. Of course, Scripture is much more than that: it is a living word; it is not just a historical document, but it "speaks" to the souls of those who receptively engage

it—and it yields ever greater riches the more frequently and
deeply we pray with it. We also come to know Jesus by learning from others who have forged intimate relationships with
Him; Christians will want to read what others, especially the
saints, have come to know about Christ.

But, again, we do not want just to learn about Jesus so we
can know about Him; we want to become one with Him; we
want to share the unity with Him wherein His thoughts are
our thoughts and our thoughts are His thoughts; our joys and
sorrows are His, and His joys and sorrows are ours.

Simply "resting" in Christ, spending time with Him
wherein He simply delights in us and we delight in Him, is
one of the pinnacles of a Christian's earthly life, an experience that, for some, is rare and wonderful and for others, is
nearly constant. The sense of having a rock upon which to
steady one's self, the sense of being loved by an unconditional
lover, the sense of participating in a joy that is transcendent
and eternal cannot last forever in this vale of tears, but it can
sustain us amidst our travails, can give us guidance and hope.

*"Developing a taste for prayer is probably the first and foremost
battle of our age."*[10]

Of course, seminarians will need lots of training in prayer
techniques. Too many people think of contemplation as a
time for introspection and "getting in touch with one's self."
That will, undoubtedly, happen; but it is not the goal and if
sought as a goal will make it impossible to achieve the goal
of union with Christ. People in academia generally have a difficult time with contemplation because it requires being able
to shut down one's searching, analytic abilities and being able
to be receptive to the truth that God wishes to share with
this person, at this time. In the classroom, seminarians will be

taught analytical skills but will need to put them aside in order to contemplate. What they have learned can certainly be beneficial "raw material" that the Holy Spirit can use to enhance and deepen their prayer life; but, again, it can be an obstacle to receptive prayer. Those with an intellectual bent need to be instructed in the difference between analytical thought and receptive prayer. They would likely benefit in ways that do not begin with words and conceptions, such as praying with an icon.

While intellectuals have a problem with moving away from abstract truths, people of our time often have a problem with any truth that is not rooted directly in their own experience. This is one of the reasons why promoting contemplation is essential to helping Christians really appropriate their faith. Since intellectual conviction that God exists, a conviction based upon philosophical or theological reasoning, is nearly impossible to obtain today—and, again, is not always the best foundation for contemplation—contemplation becomes ever more important. Contemplation enables individuals to experience Jesus' presence intimately and in a way tailored uniquely to them. That experience does not pass the test of scientifically replicated experiments so over-valued in our time; but when it brings great peace, joy, and a sense of being loved unconditionally, it exercises an authoritative grasp over our being.

For the purposes of contemplation, an excellent practice is praying; nothing is better, it seems, than the practice of *lectio divina*, a practice described beautifully by Sarah:

> *Lectio divina* is never solely our own reading. It feeds on the interpretation of those who have preceded us. The

monk, the priest, and the deacon are accustomed to it by the Divine Office itself, which has them listen to the Holy Book and then afterward to the commentaries by the Fathers of the Church. . . . if we persevere in *lectio divina* and silent listening to what the Spirit is saying to the Churches, our effort will be rewarded by unheard of jewels and riches.[11]

Seminarians not only need to be given time to participate in contemplation but must also be instructed in how to settle into contemplation and to have a fruitful experience of it. It is very wise to build their practice of it on the praying of the Divine Office, an obligation of their future lives as priests.

"The words in a homily are not a lesson: they are the echo of the words of the Master as he taught on the roads of Galilee. And so, priests must prepare their homilies in the silence of prayer and contemplation."[12]

Every priest wants to be an inspired homilist. There is no other way to be such than to draw inspiration from the practice of contemplation. Even those priests who are gifted at drawing great wisdom from ordinary and extraordinary experience need to know what wisdom to look for; their wisdom must always be that of Jesus, and that is found in contemplation.

"Whoever belongs to God hears the words of God" (Jn 8:47).

Contemplation—and here, I am referring to the high-grade contemplation facilitated by Eucharistic adoration—provides not only the opportunity to get to "know" the Divine but also to learn to hear God's voice. In fact, I suspect one of the greatest "skills" needed by a Christian is the "skill" of hearing God's voice—not just the voice of God that we hear through Scripture and the Church, but the voice of God each of us can hear in our hearts if we sufficiently clear them of all the debris that gathers there.

"I cannot do anything on my own; I judge as I hear, and my judgment is just, because I do not seek my own will but the will of the one who sent me" (Jn 5:30).

Of all the incontrovertible truths of the universe, perhaps the most important one is the truth that "God's will is better than my will." The realization of that truth is an astonishing and liberating moment in a person's life. We spend so much of our lives trying to achieve the goods that we want, to come to realize that we likely do not know what goods we should be seeking or how best to achieve those goods is an extremely sobering and daunting thought. We are confused, weak, and wretched creatures; and as soon as we recognize that condition, we can no longer be confident that shaping our lives in accord with our own thoughts and desires has much promise for leading us to the happiness we so pursue with ache-filled yearning and, perhaps, with ever increasing hopelessness.

"My sheep hear my voice; I know them, and they follow me" (Jn 10:27).

When we discover that we live in a muddled darkness and hardly know where to turn, learning or remembering that God is our Father who loves us beyond measure provides a glimmer of hope. Logic demands that we admit that an all-loving, all-knowing God knows better what is good for us than we do. Those who have some self-awareness, who have made some self-defeating and self-destructive choices, who have been seduced by the deceptive lures of the pleasures of this world, do not find it demeaning to become the sheepish

follower of the clear-sighted, sure-footed shepherding
of Christ.

*"This is my beloved Son, with whom I am well pleased; listen to
him"* (Mt 17:5).

We desperately want to know: how does God make His
path known to us? How can we know we are following Him
and not our own very imperfect ideas of what is best for us,
of what He wants from us? We do well, of course, to foster
a love for and adherence to the Church Jesus founded for we
know that through the Church, we learn how to worship; we
have access to the healing and sanctifying graces of the Sacraments, and we possess a set of carefully reasoned, strongly
justified, and clearly articulated teachings on moral matters.
All of that is a rock and a refuge in this tumultuous world in
which we live.

"Good teacher, what must I do to inherit eternal life?" (Lk 18:18)

But all those are generic; they are universal; they apply
to and serve all—and do so wonderfully. Yet each one of us,
each individual, is a unique person whose story is different
from the story of every other person who has ever lived, a
person that God created to be an unrepeatable instantiation
of some facet of His infinite beauty and goodness. God
does not want exactly the same thing for me that He wants
for everyone else; He has something gloriously spectacular
designed just for me. How do I discover what that is?

*"Oh, that today you would hear his voice: Do not harden not your
hearts"* (Ps 95:7-8).

We can learn God's plan for us only by learning to hear
God's "voice," a voice that sometimes is vocal, loud, and clear
but more often is low, subtle, and soft, for it is a lover's voice
that does not demand and insist but that loves to surprise his

beloved and cajole her into wrapping her very soul around his. How sad it is not to be able to hear that voice, either because of hardness of heart or because we have not worked to be able to distinguish that voice from all others around us.

"Yes, people of Zion, dwelling in Jerusalem, you shall no longer weep; He will be most gracious to you when you cry out; as soon as he hears he will answer you. The Lord will give you bread in adversity and water in affliction. No longer will your Teacher hide himself, but with your own eyes you shall see your Teacher, And your ears shall hear a word behind you: 'This is the way; walk in it,' when you would turn to the right or the left" (Is 30:19-21).

There are very practical reasons for learning to hear God's voice. After all, the conscience is described as the "sanctuary" where we are "alone with God whose voice echoes in [our] depths."[13] The conscience does not just remind us to obey the Commandments. We should be consulting it for all the decisions of our lives, decisions that must take place in the murky, messy places of life. Most of us would do well to constantly be asking God: "What do you want me to do next?" even when it is, more or less, perfectly obvious: the practice keeps us very connected to the Divine. It allows for "promptings of the Holy Spirit" that lift our gaze from the immediate demands of our lives.

Moreover, we face many puzzling choices that do not at all admit easy answers. We can be opposed to the spouse our child has chosen but be confused about how to respond to that choice and whether or not to go to the wedding. We can be confused about which charitable projects should be the object of our funds and times. Ignatian rules of discernment, of course, are extremely helpful and should be much more commonly taught; those who spend serious time in contemplation are able to employ those rules more accurately. Most importantly, those who spend serious time in contemplation will learn to hear God's voice.

In fact, prayer in front of the Blessed Sacrament is spectacularly efficacious for making difficult decisions even for those not practiced in contemplative prayer. A priest who works with wayward and defiant young people told me he would send unruly young persons (even Protestants) to spend time in front of the tabernacle and to ask God what He thought of their behavior. They regularly came out feeling chastened and repentant. I have found it helpful to send those contemplating doing immoral things, such as using in vitro fertilization to achieve a pregnancy, to pray about it in front of the Blessed Sacrament. They invariably make the right decision. The Blessed Sacrament is a powerful instructor to those who are open to hearing God's voice. Even those who are resistant to God's voice may benefit from the invitation to pray in from of the Blessed Sacrament. Few who are involved in sin—such as cohabitants—will take up the invitation to spend time in front of the Blessed Sacrament and to ask Jesus if he approves of their choices. I believe few go because they know what they would hear, but I believe making the invitation is still salutary: it likely pricks their consciences to make that bad choice; and, perhaps, the troubled conscience may lead eventually to a conversion.

From now on, man and god are in league, because they have the same heart and the same eyes: what God sees and hears, the believer can also see and hear. I daresay that such a love exists.[14]

Seeing God's face, being in a spousal relationship with Jesus, resting on Jesus' chest, and hearing God's voice are all what contemplation promises are goods in themselves and also means to other goods. Finding refuge in the heart of Jesus can be the only sure antidote to a world awash in evil, in idle entertainment, in noise, in pain, and that promises false security. Hearts united to Jesus can only be beacons of clarity and sources of consolation to those who possess them and who encounter them. The desire to be such is at the heart of every seminarian; contemplation advances him in that goal.

NOTES

1.   Fr. Thomas Dubay holds that the heights of contemplative prayer are in the grasp of all; *Fire Within: St Theresa of Avila, St John of the Cross, and the Gospel on Prayer* (San Francisco: Ignatius Press, 1990).

2.   Ralph Martin, *The Fulfillment of All Desire: A Guidebook for the Journey to God Based on the Wisdom of the Saints* (Steubenville, OH: Emmaus Road Publishing, 2006).

3.   Robert Cardinal Sarah, *The Power of Silence: Against the Dictatorship of Noise* (San Francisco: Ignatius Press, 2017).

4.   Anonymous, *In Sinu Jesu: When Heart Speaks to Heart—The Journal of a Priest at Prayer* (New York: Angelico Press, 2016).

5.   Sarah, 54.

6.   Ibid., 22.

7.   Ibid., 89.

8.   Ibid., 24.

9.   Ibid.

10.   Ibid., 76.

11.   Ibid., 240.

12.   Ibid., 128.

13.   Paul VI, *Gaudium et Spes* (1965), sec. 16.

14.   Sarah, 89.

LOUIS BOUYER ON THE ICONIC WAY OF SEEING: IMPLICATIONS FOR CLERICAL FORMATION

KEITH LEMNA

The vast body of theological writings of the French oratorian Louis Bouyer presents in its totality a uniquely integrated work in which Scripture, Liturgy, spirituality, and theology are ever intertwined.[1] It communicates a unified vision of the Mystery of Christ and His Church with the ultimate purpose of helping to enable the very contemplation that tends to the realization of "Christ in [us], the hope for glory" (Col 1:27). The whole of his theology is ordered to the promotion of Christian contemplation, clarifying its true nature and showing the link between the speculative endeavor in theology and the life of prayer.

Bouyer's writings contain warnings and precautions, as well. They turn us away from false paths, from habits of life or even theological styles that are not conducive to contemplation. There are many ways in which his insights can help theologians and seminary formators to think more deeply about obstacles to Christian contemplation in the wider culture and how those obstacles might be overcome in the training of seminarians. An overarching theme in his writings that is pertinent to this topic is the clarification he provides of the distinction between idolatrous and iconic ways of seeing.

Modern Idolatry and the Liberated Image

Bouyer diagnoses our modern and contemporary situation most fully in his monograph on cosmology, *Cosmos: The World and the Glory of God*, wherein he addresses the question of the origin of technological society and the way that it has dulled our capacity for Christian contemplation.[2] As the title indicates, the book is deeply concerned with theological aesthetics in a cosmological register. It is evocative of C. S. Lewis's *The Abolition of Man*, which is no accident, as Bouyer had, by the time he wrote *Cosmos*, immersed himself in the writings of the Inklings, including Lewis. He was the first person in France to review J. R. R. Tolkien's *The Lord of the Rings*, and he developed over time a writer's friendship with Tolkien as well as a properly scholarly interest in the wider work of Tolkien and his eminent academic and literary confreres.[3] The Inklings confirmed for him what he had learned in his lifelong study of John Henry Newman of the irreducible importance of human imagination and real assent; and they helped to persuade him that the problem of faith and reason in the modern age concerns, at a fundamental level, a conflict between faith and imagination.[4] In *Cosmos*, he assesses the modern age in terms of the dignity it accords—or not—to imagination, which he associates with the power of aesthetic perception, or with the contemplative intellect informed by living faith.[5] He issues withering, yet precise, critiques of the modern vitiation of humanity's perception of the Divine

Glory reflected in creation. At the same time, he expresses hope for the healing and elevation of imagination and shows that there are signs in our midst of its reaffirmation in a transformed mode.

How did our vision become occluded to the Divine Glory in the way that has happened? I can only provide the briefest outline here of Bouyer's genealogy of decline in this matter. In *Cosmos* and elsewhere, the oratorian/theologian implicitly juxtaposes idolatrous to iconic modes of seeing; and his genealogy of the process that led to this occlusion is put within the context of description of these radically different ways of setting the human gaze.[6] Modern idolatry is not, according to Bouyer, the result of an import onto Christian soil of some exotic form of religiosity. Christians themselves bear blame for falling away from true worship and enabling the conditions that have made a-religious modes of human existence more prevalent than ever before in history.[7] If Christian revelation at last actualized a transformative, iconic mode of perception, Christian religion is, nevertheless, prone to its own idolatries which, given how far there is to fall after Christ has come and elevated us to the heights of true worship, become the worst forms of religious decadence. The idolatries inherent to modern secularism and the technological mindset that is inimical to contemplation embody the principle that the corruption of the best is the worst corruption of all (*corruptio optimi pessima*).[8] Christians themselves bear blame for the construction of a culture that can so often seem to deaden our desire for contemplation of God and of creation in the light of His Glory.

The French oratorian tells a story of decline and fall within the lives of the faithful themselves that began in the late Middle Ages, concomitant with or even preceding the advent of theological or philosophical nominalism. Nominalist theological and philosophical currents provided intellectual justifications for a culture that found it increasingly difficult to take seriously, in its daily existence, ascetical discipline in the practice of faith. Bouyer describes here the era of the rise of the bourgeoisie, of the money-seeking class that turned away from the monastic ideal of Christian life. Voluntary poverty, if understood as a concretely embodied condition of life, lost its universal prestige within Christian culture among Christians themselves as paradigmatic for giving witness to the faith.[9]

This had an impact on the intellectual life of the Church on the deepest level. Methods of scriptural exegesis were altered. In an increasingly materialistic culture, exegesis increasingly degenerated into a biblical literalism that collapsed the levels of meaning of the scriptural text (literal, allegorical, tropological, and anagogical) onto a single plane. As people were paying more attention to the physical things of this world—without reference to God—than to God or to the world in God, a mindset developed that gave precedence to the formal expression of faith over its object. If, in light of Aquinas's *analogia entis*, theologians would be able to articulate the difference between the object of faith and its conceptual expression, the new mentality produced theologies of univocity in which concepts and formulas, human representations, were accorded the status of Divine revelation itself.[10]

Aquinas's approach to Scripture, like that of the Church Fathers, realized the four senses of the biblical Word in an existential exegesis inseparable from growth in the spiritual life.[11] The believer grows in knowledge and love of God by participation in the life of God in and through the Mystical Body of Christ, of which he or she is a member, prolonging, thereby, the Incarnation centered on the Paschal Mystery. The spiritual senses of Scripture, grasped in the ever-increasing perfection of the spiritual life, formulate and deepen the literal meaning which—although it can only be speculatively grasped in and through concepts—is, nevertheless, irreducible to particular concepts.[12] The mystical meanings of Scripture point to the unity of the Divine design for our salvation in the Incarnation of Christ, at last reaching in the anagogical meaning toward the eschatological fulfillment of our life together with Christ in the grace of the Spirit. This existential exegesis, Bouyer argues, was increasingly ignored by theologians at the end of the Middle Ages in the quest for scientific objectivity in theological utterance. Bouyer speaks of a consequent loss of sense of the organic unity of the mystery of faith, with the Christian intellectual life splintered "into a multitude of disjointed or heterogeneous propositions that could lead only to the perception of a shattered world . . . a downright irreligious vision of the whole of reality . . . affecting the very heart of faith."[13]

The end result of the process that Bouyer describes is the procedure of so-called "anthropological reduction" that was common in modernity but that had its roots in nominalism and materialistic praxis.[14] This reduction makes human experience, in its shifting social configurations, the ground of credibility for the faith and the measure of its propositions. The type of theology operative in the regime of anthropological reduction attempted to give meaning to the assertions of faith by seeing:

in them merely a particular formulation, of indifferent
value in itself, of the spontaneous convictions which in
any case he [modern man] harbors, and which are his as
long as he remains sincere and faithful to his own truth;
for each modern man, indeed, there can be . . . no truth
that is not precisely his.[15]

Human experience was, thus, increasingly understood
counter to the centrifugal intentionality necessary to heed the
call of the Divine Word who alone can transform us in the
perfection of Christian life. It was reduced to a protean and
unaccountable interiority.

The self-enclosed self, sometimes called the "buffered
self," screened off from contemplation of the Divine Glory,
became sovereign. Bouyer traces, up to a certain historical
point, the unfolding cultural logic of the idolatrous society
created by the sovereign self. He assesses its consequences
(and not only in *Cosmos*) in terms of various idolatries: power,
technology, mass transportation, sexual gratification, as well
as philosophical or theological concepts. In all of this, he recognizes that there is a problem of the image and, therefore,
of the imagination. Rather than seeing ourselves as created
in the image of the Divine, we seek to refashion creation
according to our untransformed selfhood, with its guiding
representations and self-referential images, idols that issue
forth from the imagination in conjunction with aspirations of
the will lowered by modern materialism.[16] However, Bouyer
did not directly assess the most recent stage in the process of
this unfolding cultural logic. I refer to what has been called
the "society of the spectacle," with its "liberated image"
freed from an archetypal, measuring presence transcendent to
human desire.[17]

One of Bouyer's most eminent spiritual children, the contemporary French philosopher and theologian Jean-Luc Marion, has directly explored this new terrain in his essays collected in the book *The Crossing of the Visible* and, in the fashion of Bouyer, proposes the way of the icon as a remedy to its various idolatries.[18] There is, in some respects (if not all), deep congruence between Marion's work on the topic of the "liberated image" and Bouyer's genealogy of decline and fall in *Cosmos*; and so, I turn to Marion briefly to conclude this first section.

Marion's essays presume the sinful presence of consumerism in our midst, in connection with a technocratic mindset, a connection whose proto-existence in early modernity Bouyer outlines in *Cosmos*. Modern technique, Marion argues, especially targeting the "televisual image," has sundered the image from every original or prototype, giving it a self-subsistent, wholly immanent existence within the confines of the screen. We are willfully screened-in by a constant barrage of images on the television screen that admit of no spatio-temporal limitation. We are "opened" to a false infinity that is, in fact, a type of enclosure. Appearance gains precedence over being: to be is to be seen.[19] The appearance of the image on the screen is oftentimes more real to us, or more important, than the flesh and blood realities in our midst. If Marion confines his comments in *The Crossing of the Visible* to "televisual images," his analysis is, nevertheless, quite pertinent to our era of internet and smartphones. The mobility of the smart-phone, especially, enables the screened-in image to be with us everywhere. Unlike with the televisual image, or with the images on a desktop computer, we no longer have to set aside a special quasi-sacred space for viewing the image that governs our lives. The fallen sacrality of the techno-visual image blankets the earth, in the sense that it covers over the "given-ness" of natural reality.

Why do these images, freed from governing, transcendent exemplars, so entrance us? The modern, "liberated image," Marion explains, is measured by the tastes of the ones who view it. The appetite of the viewer or spectator who gazes upon it for the sole pleasure of seeing is the absolute norm. "[E]very image," Marion says, "must reproduce in itself the measure of a desire."[20] This is the essence of idolatry, as Marion describes it, that influences the whole of our way of seeing. The American theologian Norman Wirzba, who follows Marion closely on this subject, summarizes the point:

> [Idolatry] is a form of perception (and thus also a capacity for apprehension) in which what is seen reflects the ambition, anxiety, insecurity, hubris—the deep desire—of the one perceiving. To gaze at things idolatrously is to put in motion ways of naming and narration—and thus also practical and economic forms of engagement with the world—that establish us as the centers and bestowers of value and significance. This is why Jean-Luc Marion says idols function as mirrors reflecting the scope of the viewer's aim. In an idolatrous context we cannot see things as they are. We see them for what we desire them to be.[21]

The idolatrous mode of perception that is endemic to modern consumerism, technique, and the contemporary regime of the liberated image is obviously antithetical to true contemplation, in which the human gaze is determined and led by an Other. Yet, many of us are habitually ensnared by the image that conforms to our desires. It is all too easy on our attention. How can we overcome this ensnarement or addiction—or smash the ubiquitous golden calf, the image that renders contemplation so foreign to our habits? The attitude of the iconoclast might seem to recommend itself to us. It might seem that a proper response would require the destruction of images and the rejection of the imagination that enables their production; but this is certainly not what Bouyer recommends—although on this point, there may well be a subtle difference between Bouyer and Marion.[22] Rather, for Bouyer, we require transformation in the iconic mode of perception or imagination and recognizing anew the importance and true meaning of icons. The image has to be liberated anew in a true and lasting liberation: tethered now to the One who alone is the "image of the invisible God" (Col 1:15), the ultimate Exemplar of the image, who alone renders it meaningful.

Mystical Unity and Iconic Imagination

What can a theologian do in a seminary setting to help to encourage a properly iconic imagination or way of seeing, to get out of the hall of mirrors of the liberated image, as we know it, in the civilization of the sovereign self, to enter into Christian contemplation? Bouyer's envisioning of the proper task or approach of theology can help us with this question. We have seen that for Bouyer, modern modes of idolatry are rooted in practices for which theologies or philosophies become enterprises of justification. Still, he recognizes that ways of doing theology can offer more or less encouragement to spiritual contemplation and overturning of the idolatrous image in favor of the iconic image.

Idolatry bespeaks polytheism and the multiplication of gods. The biblical rejection of the idol follows necessarily from the revelation of the one transcendent God to us, who alone is able to touch us in our deepest immanence. Theology itself must reflect the Divine unity as a discipline integrated around the figure of Christ, who is the plenitude of God's revelation. No one in mid-twentieth century theology was more to the forefront than Bouyer in making this case for unity, which impacted the Second Vatican Council. Bouyer's work, beginning with his highly-influential 1945 publication *The Paschal Mystery*, was important in showing especially the need to overcome the sundering of theology and praxis, so that our unity in belief in the triune God might shine forth more fully not only in presenting the Divine Mystery but in the conjunction between our words and deeds as theologians.[23]

This brings me to the first of four concrete suggestions that I want to make with regard to theology and contemplation, based on Bouyer's writings: theology needs intrinsic integration with spirituality and liturgy. There is a distinctive lesson to be derived from Bouyer's work in this regard—which Marion has, in fact, clarified in a striking way, showing the uniqueness of Bouyer's work. In an intervention at a conference on Bouyer in Paris in 2016, Marion compared Bouyer's approach to dogmatic theology with that of other famous twentieth century theologians.[24] He asked what serves as the guiding principle or intrinsic norm for theological inquiry for these theologians, taken individually, and this is how he identified the singular mark of Bouyer's work. For Karl Rahner, Marion says, the logical, philosophical concept is the norm, while for Karl Barth, the concept, while normative, is understood in accordance with the Lutheran logic of the Divine Word, the kerygma as event, which can lead theology in different directions, such as that taken by Rudolf Bultmann. Hans Urs von Balthasar, Marion claims, seems not to take the concept but the figure as normative. This puts him very close to Bouyer. Nevertheless, Marion suggests, he develops the figure in a fully conceptual way in his *Theo-dramatics* and *Theo-logic*, which Bouyer does not do in his writings. The concept remains normative as the leading thread in dogmatic theology for Henri de Lubac, Yves Congar, and Marie-Dominique Chenu, O.P., in order to deconstruct the *aporias* of contemporary theology by transposing the present into the past in an ambitious hermeneutical effort to reset our theological direction toward the future. For Jean Daniélou, the norm of theology is the conceptual, philological foundation laid by the Church Fathers in the first ten centuries.[25]

Marion says that Bouyer's guiding norm is different from all of these. It is not the concept but liturgical and spiritual practice that guides his theoretical and historical theology (which were comprehensive) and this, from the very beginning of it and all the way through. Contemplative practice, in the corporate life of prayer of the Church, is not only the intended issuance of his theology but its foundation and manifest DNA. The theological concept, though recognized as necessary, is always contextualized in Bouyer's work by the embodied practice of prayer. Marion concludes that Bouyer is uniquely lucid on this point, and this is why, he says, "Bouyer will remain one of the masters of theology to come, because his method is first practicable . . . freest of all presuppositions… [and] safer in the sense that it is based directly on the daily practice of the Church."[26]

So, if we follow Bouyer, we should recognize that theology is indissociable from the life and experience of the Church, centered in the concrete practice of Eucharistic worship. It can only be what it should be when surrounded and informed by the liturgical event, where alone the theologian can receive the Divine Word, enlivened and transformed in charity by the gift of the Holy Spirit. The only authentic theology not only leads to spirituality but is animated from the beginning by a liturgically-formed spiritual dynamism. Marion did not mention any Eastern Orthodox theologians in his intervention, but I suggest that Bouyer's approach to theology may, more than that of any other twentieth century Western theologian—while remaining very much fully Western and even scientific—resemble that of the most eminent Eastern Orthodox theologians of the era such as Vladimir Lossky or Dumitru Stăniloae, whose works on dogmatic theology are suffused with liturgical spirituality.[27]

Another way of putting this, I think, is that for Bouyer, dogmatic theology should not fear to be closely joined with "mystical theology." In fact, he insisted on this point. Christianity is *the* great mystery, he said, "the Mystery of unity and life, of the organic unity of the true life: the life of God in Himself, seen, as the Fathers had seen it, as the source of life and charity in the Church, the life of the love of truth, of a truth which is a truth of love."[28] The foundation of all true theology is the Mystery of Christ opening to us through the Incarnation the eternal love of the Holy Trinity in the sacraments of faith. Theology must be careful not to dissolve the unity of this Mystery into a congeries of disconnected mysteries. A truly mystical theology is inherently ordered to a wider formation in knowledge by way of practice, by development in union and assimilation into Christ. Bouyer certainly held that all theology should maintain this mystical character, even when it engages in scientific dialogue and exposition. *Cosmos* is a confluence of mysticism or spirituality and science in the broadest meaning of the term *scientia*, bringing the two together in a way that is surely unique in modern thought. But the mystical or sacramental character of faith is a connecting thread running through the whole of Bouyer's dogmatics and even fundamental theology. Mystical or—perhaps, better said—"liturgical theology" is not a field set apart for Bouyer. It is the framework for his scientific investigations and speculative expostulations. It even reaches, for him, into the domain of philosophy.[29]

My second suggestion, which is really a corollary of the first, is that theology needs to place a greater value on symbols and symbolism. Bouyer said this expressly, and his work on the economy of salvation presents the argument that the Divine Word gives Himself to us by taking up, healing, and transfiguring natural religious symbols.[30] What is the precise character of this transfiguration? So much of Bouyer's work seeks to answer this question, recognizing that the symbol is basic and irreducible, and that theology and economy are mediated in the realm of the symbol. There is no other way for the Eternal Word to be received by us in our humanity except through the sacred word, image, and action. There is a presentational necessity in this regard. God does not give Himself to us, first and foremost, by means of a pure concept, understood as a clear, distinct, abstract idea. Our intelligence is applied to knowledge of the sensible and can only be elevated to the spiritual plane on the basis of the sensible to which it must return.

Bouyer emphasizes that the symbol is not reducible to a primitive, infantile form of expression of human realities. We do not simply surpass the symbol by means of the pure concept in order, at last, to accede to the truth of human, cosmic, and Divine reality.[31] Theology, in the Bouyerian perspective, must always be attentive to the symbol, for instance, in sacramental theology, exploring the meaning of the use of water in Baptism, or the elements in the Eucharist, or, in Trinitarian theology—seemingly the most conceptual and speculative of all the theological disciplines—giving greater attention to the Trinitarian symbols in Scripture, liturgy, and iconography.[32] Likewise, in dogmatic Christology, Bouyer argues that we need to recover and develop a proper theology of the image.[33]

Theology, then, if we learn from Bouyer, should be guided by what Avery Dulles referred to as an "ecclesial-transformative" method, which emphasizes that revelation is not given to us, first and foremost, through propositional discourse but through "the life and worship of the Church."[34] In *The Craft of Theology*, Dulles distinguishes between three approaches to theology on the basis of how they assess the symbol. The first approach, the propositional-cognitive approach of Neo-Scholasticism, in which Dulles was himself trained, subordinates symbols to propositional speech. Symbols are taken to illustrate, for the benefit of sense and imagination, what can only truly be grasped by discursive reason. The second approach, the experiential-expressivism of liberal Protestantism, holds that symbols of faith are projections or constructions of human consciousness, issuing forth from the transformative action of God on the human spirit. This is, of course, corollary to the anthropological reduction described above; and it tends to historicize and psychologize the symbol. The third approach, the ecclesial-transformative type of theology, holds that symbols have depth or fullness of meaning that transcends the powers of discursive or conceptual reasoning to grasp in fullness:

> A symbol, in this perspective, is a perceptible sign that evokes a realization of that which surpasses ordinary objective cognition. Symbolic knowledge is self-involving, for the symbol "speaks to us only insofar as it lures us to situate ourselves mentally within the universe of meaning and value which it opens to us."[35]

Bouyer's work is an example of "ecclesial-transformative" theology; and if he was, as Marion suggests, particularly lucid on the matter, he was hardly all alone. In fact, the text that is the *locus classicus* for the recovery of this approach to the symbol is chapter ten of Henri de Lubac's *Corpus Mysticum*, entitled "From Symbolism to Dialectic."[36] A more symbolic type of theology is better able, de Lubac argued, to appreciate the levels of depth in the Divine Mystery communicated to us in revelation and, so, is more naturally attuned to a contemplative type of rationality. He refers to the ontology of the symbol in the Church Fathers as founding a theology that is always a "religious contemplation of the mysteries."[37] This type of theology is not without its own proper rigor and does not liberate theologians from the need to develop concepts, but it does set them on an open path, in that it helps them to realize that their conceptual expressions can never constitute altogether a perfect, fixed set.

The third suggestion I have, following directly from this second point, has to do with the importance of imagination and the image. Bouyer frequently refers to the importance of "imagination" as it was understood by Schelling, Wordsworth, Coleridge—and especially, Newman.[38] He tends to associate "imagination" with "poetic intuition" or "mythopoetic thinking," as well as with the *nous* or *intellectus* distinguished by the Church Fathers and Scholastic theologians from *dianoia* or *ratio*, that is, "discursive reasoning." Josef Pieper summarized well the difference:

> *Ratio* is the power of discursive thought, or searching and re-searching, abstracting, refining and concluding whereas *intellectus* refers to the ability of "simply looking" (*simplex intuitus*), to which the truth presents itself as a landscape to the eye. The spiritual knowing power of the human mind, as the ancients understood it, is really two things in one: *ratio* and *intellectus*: all knowing involved both. The path of discursive reasoning is accompanied and penetrated by the *intellectus'* untiring vision, which is not active but passive, or better, receptive—a receptively operating power of intellect.[39]

Bouyer argued that modernity, following certain lines of Neo-Scholastic thought, separated *ratio* from *intellectus* in order to achieve clear and distinct ideas that are uniform and that do not deceive in the way that the symbol is presumed to do. He swam in the waters of those thinkers who distinguished a "higher reason" and sought its validation in order to overcome this distortion.

Connected with a turn to imagination is a turn to the unique concreteness of the iconic image. Bouyer advocated for iconography as a crucial dimension of Christian thought and practice and suggested that dogmatic theology needs to be informed by a sense or feel for the meaning of the icon, which is the imprint of the invisible God in the face of the incarnate Lord.[40] Reading Bouyer on the icon, one recognizes how important it is for Christians to receive and communicate in full the implications of the theology and spirituality of the Second Council of Nicaea. Theology needs to embrace the iconic image in the manner of its kenotic presentation of Christ in the flesh, who "[empties] himself, taking the form of a slave" (Phil 2:7).

In *The Truth of Icons*, Bouyer argues that the icon, and a proper theology of the icon, is needed to communicate the depths and implications of the Eucharist. There is a close connection between traditional belief in the Eucharist and the veneration of holy images. Iconography is the expression of faith in the sacramentality of the Divine Word as cultic word and is needed to reform our gaze, to break us from our habitual, idolatrous tendency to project ourselves onto the world and make our own image the measure of the real. The icon, Bouyer shows, uniquely deploys inverse perspective, giving the impression that what it depicts converges toward the one who contemplates it.[41] The icon institutes a unique "counter-experience" or "counter-intentionality," where we recognize that everything we are is given to us by God who is one of us, yet transcendent, kenotically present in the human face of the Son. We receive ourselves in receiving the gaze of the ultimate Other who has made Himself one of us in our very flesh. The renewed interest in the icon in recent decades is a providential development assisting the Church in bringing succor to those wounded by the society of the spectacle and the idolatrous, liberated image. Christian contemplation requires breaking through the shackles that we place on ourselves in obedience to the liberated image. We need the iconic image, with its Trinitarian counter-intentionality, more and more.

There is much more that could be said about this topic. The icon is essential to the development of mystical theology. The icon presents the crowning image to our imagination and penetrates it with a transcendent light. The imagination is stimulated in a special way by the icon, which calls forth the spiritual world in the sensible domain.[42] Habituation into perception of the icon can convert and heal the imagination. The meaning of the "way of the icon" can be extended into how we approach the sacred texts of the Catholic Tradition in the classroom, as James Keating has shown.[43] There is an iconic way of reading, whereby we do not simply come to know and love God in and through the text but to be known and loved by Him. Theology can more or less attest to the counter-intentionality of the iconic way of seeing, the form of perception that flows from the propagation in us of the Mystery of Christ in His Death and Resurrection.

Fourth and lastly, Bouyer stresses the need for purification and renunciation as a necessary dimension of Christian formation, particularly with respect to voluntary, evangelical poverty; and I want to dwell on this point briefly in conclusion and insist with him on its importance in forming seminarians, as well as forming seminarian formators.[44] The three previous points give suggestions for classroom content and approach: integrating theology and spirituality, giving the symbols of faith their due, and communicating the theology and spirituality of the Second Council of Nicaea, which should have an impact on Christology, Trinitarian theology, theological anthropology, and even fundamental theology. However, this other suggestion takes us beyond the classroom.

Bouyer wrote much on spirituality, showing the need for purification of our passions and desires if we are to see all things with the eyes of faith, to see the world in the Word as God Himself sees it, with God's own eyes, as Christian contemplation enables us to do. Bouyer stressed that we cannot perceive the beauty of creation reflecting the glory of God, or of the Divine image in our neighbor or in ourselves, without ascetical purification. Truly, this is absolutely essential to all programs of Christian formation. Regarding priestly formation, Bouyer argued that it has a link to the monastic way of formation in that, in a first stage, renunciation and separation from the world are requirements. In order to save the world, we must first renounce it in its fallen condition. In order to exercise his spiritual paternity in the world through and in his apostolic life, the priest must first learn to withdraw from the world. This was a common understanding in seminary formation in Bouyer's day and might need some recovery in our own.

Although we are not all called to the vows of religious life, we are all called to live them, at least temporarily, in ways that befit our state in life. Of the three evangelical counsels, Bouyer argues, poverty is basic and includes within it the other vows, which are applications of it to the whole of life. Poverty frees us from enslavement to the world, the "world" understood here, as in John's Gospel, as the organization of all things in divergence from the logic of God's plan or wisdom.[45] Clerical poverty, poverty in an active form, enables greater actualization of the priest's exercise of spiritual paternity. Surely, even if it is not monastic poverty, it requires simplicity of life and the development of a new mindset, a new of way of perceiving, an instinct or imagination that readily acknowledges the beauty and joy of renunciation for the sake of the Kingdom. This mindset or way of perceiving is not always apparent in priests, religious, or in Catholic laity, as we all know, so it is hardly trivial to assert its importance as well as its Gospel credentials.

Drawing together the unity of experience in a deeply sacramental theology centered on the Mystery of Christ, keeping a balanced harmony of theology and economy, commending the transformation of our gaze in the mode of iconic counter-experience, Bouyer, at the same time, teaches us, in the line of the Church Fathers, how important our way of life is to the way in which we see. We cannot contemplate God without the life of Christian, evangelical poverty. This enables us to overcome the reign of the lower desires over our lives. Surely, we who are seminary formators should model material simplicity in our lives. How else can we ourselves be liberated from the society of the spectacle, an outcome of the consumerism that Bouyer castigates in *Cosmos*? We all have need of seeing anew, seeing with new eyes, with a gaze transformed by the gaze of Christ; but this cannot be accomplished without renunciation in the community of the Church, without Christian asceticism; and we all have to take up the Cross in this regard.

There are certain things that seminary formators can do to encourage recognition of the importance of material detachment. Certainly, ministry assignments are crucial. Seminarians (and formators) should get to know and work with the poor in their own geographical area. If (as sometimes happens already today) seminarians can be sent on immersion experiences among the poorest of the poor in regions of Latin America, or Appalachia, there should also be outreach programs at the local level. One might refer to these as "local immersions" among the poor. Moreover, should not teachers and formation staff themselves be involved in these forms of ministry? At any rate, our capacity for effective ministry in this regard is not something isolatable from the iconic way of seeing. If renunciation opens our gaze to the gaze of Christ that constitutes our being, our capacity for empathetic, fleshly presence to the people in our midst can only be enhanced if we are habituated to the "counter-intentionality" of the icon. We learn, thereby, to see the other in the light of God's charity and mercy. The Exemplar is present in His people. If Louis Bouyer did not himself explore the concrete implications of his own theology in this regard, his work, nevertheless, suggests these sorts of connections. His joint emphasis on contemplation of the icon and voluntary poverty tends to encourage the development of these themes in conjunction. His is an integrated view that might even help us to reconcile the tensions created by divergent emphases in the teachings of recent popes. Christian, contemplative praxis joins together presence before the liturgical icon with the ministry of mercy to all God's people; and both are necessary for the prolonging of the Incarnation in the dispensation of the Church.

NOTES

1.   See Jean Duchesne, *Louis Bouyer* (Perpignan: Éditions Artège, 2011). Duchesne provides in this book a beautiful and concise summary, in an elegant French style, of Bouyer's work in its integrative heart as well as its historical importance.

2.   Louis Bouyer, *Cosmos: The World and the Glory of God*, trans. Pierre de Fontnouvelle (Petersham, MA: St. Bede Publications, 1988)—originally published by Cerf, 1982).

3.   Michaël Devaux, "Le Problème de l'Imagination et de la Foi chez Louis Bouyer: En Lisant, En Écrivant Avec Les Inklings," in *La théologie de Louis Bouyer: Du Mystère à la Sagesse* (Paris: Parole et Silence, 2016), 141-62. Based on important archival research, Devaux details the extent of the influence of the Inklings on Bouyer, while also showing the importance of Bouyer in making the Inklings known in France.

4.   Ibid. See also Irène Fernandez, *C. S. Lewis: Mythe, Raison Ardente* (Geneva: Ad Solem, 2005), 127-215. In these pages, Fernandez masterfully expounds Lewis's critique of modern scientific abstractionism and the need to return to the mythic image. The resonances with Bouyer's thought are clear, and Devaux has explicated the concrete connections between the two thinkers.

5.   See Louis Bouyer, *Le Consolateur: Esprit-Saint et Vie de Grace* (Paris: Cerf, 1980), 372-373.

6.   See Louis Bouyer, *Vérité des Icônes: La Tradition Iconographique Chrétienne et sa Signification* (Milan: Criterion, 1984). In juxtaposing idolatrous with iconic modes of perception, I am, in fact, reading Bouyer's *Cosmos* in conjunction with this book on icons, which was published around the same time as *Cosmos*.

7.   This analysis is especially carried out in chapter 13 of *Cosmos*, 117-129. In this section, I follow especially this chapter of the book.

8.   Bouyer, *Cosmos*, 129.

9.   Ibid., 12-14.

10.   Ibid., 127-129.

11.   See Marie-Hélène Grintchenko, *Une Approche Théologique du Monde: Cosmos du Père Louis Bouyer* (Paris: Parole et Silence, 2015), 162-66. Grintchenko summarizes Bouyer's history of scriptural exegesis very concisely in these pages, and I follow her exposition in this paragraph.

12.   Bouyer argues that our knowledge is of reality in and through concepts but not of concepts themselves. He eschews the representationalist epistemologies of the modern age, which are sometimes present in modern Scholastic theories of knowledge. See Bouyer, *Cosmos*, 127-128 and 236 (note 7).

13.   Bouyer, *Cosmos*, 128.

14. See Hans Urs von Balthasar, *Love Alone is Credible*, trans. D.C. Schindler (San Francisco: Ignatius Press, 2004), 31-50. To my knowledge, Bouyer does not himself use the expression "anthropological reduction." But it is concordant with the dimension of Bouyer's analysis pertaining to the modern decline and fall. On the other hand, Balthasar, Bouyer's friend and colleague, does not (to my knowledge) explore the advent of the anthropological reduction in the light of the concrete factors of economy and practice that Bouyer describes.

15. Bouyer, *Cosmos*, 128.

16. Ibid., 16-17, 121-122.

17. See Guy Debord, *The Society of the Spectactle*, trans. Donald Nicholson-Smith (New York: Zone Books, 1994), 12. It is from this book, very influential in France from its first publication in 1967, that I get this expression.

18. See especially Jean-Luc Marion, *The Crossing of the Visible*, trans. James K.A. Smith (Palo Alto, CA: Stanford University Press, 2004), 46-87. In bringing this all-too-brief first section to a close, I shall focus on a couple of main points in these pages.

19. Ibid., 53.

20. Ibid., 51.

21. Norman Wirzba, *From Nature to Creation: A Christian Vision for Understanding and Loving Our World* (Grand Rapids, MI: Baker Academic, 2015), 68.

22. See Douglas Hedley, *The Iconic Imagination* (New York: Bloomsbury, 2016), 149-51. Hedley argues, as the title of the book suggests, for the importance of what he calls "iconic imagination." In the pages referenced in this note, he contrasts his view with that of Marion. He argues that Marion insists that the icon should replace the function of the imagination. If this is, indeed, Marion's position, the philosopher diverges from his spiritual mentor, and Bouyer would actually align more closely with Hedley than with Marion. Indeed, Hedley follows the tradition of Anglophone Christian Platonism that Bouyer so admired—with Cardinal Newman as its pre-eminent representative. So, while Marion, like Bouyer, turns to the icon to free us from the liberated image, he may do so while being insufficiently attentive to the importance of imagination.

23. Louis Bouyer, *Le Mystère Pascal: Méditation sur la Liturgie des Trois Dernier Jours de la Semaine Sainte* (Paris: Cerf, 1945; 5th edition, revised and augmented, Cerf 1954; 5th edition revised and augmented reprinted, Cerf, 2009); *The Paschal Mystery*, trans. Sister Mary Benoit (Chicago: Regnery, 1960).

24. Jean-Luc Marion, "Cinq Remarques Sur L'Originalité De L'œuvre De Louis Bouyer," Conference at Collège des Bernardins, November 9, 2016, 1-5, https://media.collegedesbernardins.fr/content/pdf/

formation/etudier-louis-bouyer/2016-11-09-6-intervention-du-pr-j-l-marion.pdf.

25. Ibid., 5.

26. Ibid.

27. See Louis Bouyer, "La Situation de la Théologie," *Communio* [French language edition] 2.1 (1977): 11-20. Bouyer is critical in this article of attempts to turn theology into an "objective" science like other modern sciences. Yet, it can hardly be denied that his work maintains a scientific, if not objectivist, character.

28. Louis Bouyer, *Newman's Vision of Faith: A Theology for Times of General Apostasy* (San Francisco: Ignatius Press, 1986), 13.

29. See especially Louis Bouyer, "Poésie, Philosophie, et Sagesse Chrétienne," unpublished manuscript, Abbey of Saint-Wandrille, Nov. 1986.

30. See especially Louis Bouyer, *Le Métier de Théologien: Entretiens Avec Georges Daix* (Geneva: Ad Solem, 2004), 109-112. These pages give Bouyer's clearest exposition of how he sees the place of the symbol in Catholic theology. He views the theology of the Church Fathers as essentially symbolic.

31. Ibid.

32. On this point, Bouyer's theology is strikingly similar to Joseph Ratzinger's. See Alcuin Reid, O.S.B., *The Organic Development of the Liturgy: The Principles of Liturgical Reform and Their Relation to the Twentieth-Century Liturgical Movement Prior to the Second Vatican Council*, 2nd ed. (San Francisco: Ignatius Press, 2005), 9-13. Bouyer and Ratzinger both agree, with respect to sacramental theology, that we should guard against, as Ratzinger says, "the wrong path up which we might be led by a Neoscholastic sacramental theology that is disconnected from the living form of the liturgy" (p. 11).

33. See Louis Bouyer, *The Eternal Son*, trans. Sister Simone Inkel and John F. Laughlin (Huntington, IN: Our Sunday Visitor Press, 1978), 416-417.

34. Avery Dulles, *The Craft of Theology: From Symbol to System* (New York: Crossroad, 2001), 18. Dulles quotes himself here.

35. Ibid., 18-19.

36. Henri de Lubac, *Corpus Mysticum: The Eucharist and the Church in the Middle Ages*, trans. Gemma Simmonds, C.J., with Richard Price and Christopher Stephens (Notre Dame: 2006), 221-247.

37. Ibid., 229.

38. See Bouyer, *Cosmos*, 161-180.

39. Quoted by Tracey Rowland, *Catholic Theology* (New York: Bloomsbury, 2017), 13. From Josef Pieper, *Leisure as the Basis of Culture* (San Francisco: Ignatius Press, 2009), 11-12.

40. Bouyer, *Vérité des Icônes*, 5-10.

41.   Bouyer, *Vérité des Icônes*, 34. Marion quotes from this page in *Crossing the Visible*, 98 (note 12): "One can rightly observe, for example, the effectiveness of inverted perspective in the alcove of Daphnée, where the Transfiguration is reproduced: it appears to push us toward our own encounter with the Christ of Glory, between the adoration of Moses and Elijah."

42.   On this point, see Charles Bernard, "Théologie Symbolique," (Paris: Téqui, 1978), 111-135. Dulles cites this work in *The Craft of Theology*, 226 (note 9).

43.   James Keating, *Resting on the Heart of Christ: The Vocation and Spirituality of the Seminary Theologian* (Omaha, NE: IPF Publications, 2009), 96-104.

44.   See Louis Bouyer, *Introduction to the Spiritual Life*, trans. Mary Perkins Ryan (Notre Dame: Christian Classics, 2013), 169-173, 241-245.

45.   Bouyer, *Introduction to Spirituality*, 176.

Cana Contemplation

Earl K. Fernandes

The new evangelization, which recent Popes have called for, does not occur in a vacuum but in a constantly changing culture. The profound changes affecting the world in which future priests are formed demand an equally profound reconsideration of how the Gospel is communicated. Central to evangelization is a lived faith that must be learned and deepened constantly, especially in prayer and contemplation. There is an urgent need for this missionary spirit as challenges in transmitting the faith are increasing rapidly.

Amid globalization, emerging technologies, and disconnectedness, a feeling of meaninglessness is growing in the lives of men and women. What the Bishops of Latin America recognized some years ago is just as pertinent today:

> Our cultural traditions are no longer handed on from one generation to the next with the same ease as in the past. This even affects that deepest core of each culture, constituted by religious experience, which is now likewise difficult to hand on through education and the beauty of cultural expressions. It even reaches into the family itself, which, as a place of dialogue and intergenerational

solidarity, had been one of the most important vehicles for handing on the faith.[1]

For this reason, the new *Ratio Fundamentalis* places strong emphasis on the propaedeutic stage of clerical formation that precedes philosophical and theological studies.[2] The *Ratio* remarks that "the appropriate involvement of the priestly ministry in the culture of today, with all the complex problems that it brings in its wake," demands not only that priests remain open and up-to-date, but also that priests "remain firmly anchored to the four dimensions of forma-tion: human, spiritual, intellectual and pastoral."[3] Elements of contemporary culture have left many seminarians in the predicament of being self-referential. Seminary formation ought to address this problem in preparation for mission as the new *Ratio* notes:

> The seminarian is called to "go out of himself", to make his way in Christ, towards the Father and towards others, embracing the call to the priesthood, dedicating himself to work with the Holy Spirit, to achieve a serene and creative interior synthesis between strength and weakness. The educational endeavor helps seminarians to bring all aspects of their personality to Christ, in this way making them consciously free for God and for others. In fact, it is only in the crucified and risen Christ that this path of integration finds meaning and completion; all things are united in him (cf. Eph 1:10), so that "God might be all in all" (cf. 1Cor 15:28).[4]

Overcoming the cultural influences that lead the seminar-ian to be self-referential requires a commitment to contem-plating the Lord, transforming the seminarian into a man of communion. The *Ratio* states: "In contemplating the Lord, who offered His life for others, he [the seminarian] will be able to give himself generously and with self-sacrifice for the People of God."[5] In these reflections, I wish to offer some thoughts about seminary formation, culture, and contemplation by focusing on the Lord and His Mother at the Wedding Feast of Cana[6], following the thought of noted Mariologist Michele G. Masciarelli.[7]

The Dynamic of Cana

It is important to observe the dynamics of the event at Cana in Galilee; there, the Lord performed the first of His signs, and the disciples saw His glory and began to believe in Him.[8] In John's Gospel, it is at Cana that Jesus is revealed as the Son of the Father. The event of Cana points to Christ. *He* is the One who *performs* the sign. He manifests *His* glory. Seeing the miracle, the disciples believe in *Him*. It is good to contemplate Cana to strengthen the faith of the seminarian and priest, who remains a disciple throughout his life.[9]

Mary's presence at Cana is not merely coincidental. The *Catechism of the Catholic Church* says:

> At Cana, the Mother of Jesus asks her son for the needs of a wedding feast; this is a sign of another feast—that of the wedding of the Lamb where he gives his body and blood at the request of the Church, his Bride. It is at the hour of the New Covenant, at the foot of the Cross, that Mary is heard as the Woman, the new Eve, the true "Mother of all the Living."[10]

Mary's presence at Cana and Calvary cannot be overlooked. At the beginning and end of John, she is directly and uniquely involved with the person and saving work of her Son. Her journey toward the Cross begins at Cana, the site of Jesus' first miracle. It is an event that prophesies of the Hour of Jesus' glorification. Just as the celebration of Epiphany allows the Church, with the Magi, to adore the Lord, so, too, the wedding feast of Cana reveals the glory of the Lord, a glory that is extended in the celebration of the Eucharist. The *Catechism* teaches:

> The sign of the water turned into wine at Cana already announces the Hour of Jesus' glorification. It makes manifest the fulfillment of the wedding feast in the Father's kingdom, where the faithful will drink the new wine that has become the Blood of Christ.[11]

The setting of the miracle of Cana at a nuptial ceremony should not be overlooked either. Cana can be understood in light of two other "nuptial" pacts that also took place "on the third day": the covenant made between the Lord and Israel at Mount Sinai[12] and the new and eternal covenant of Calvary, in which Jesus gave Himself up entirely for His Bride. At Sinai, the people exclaimed: "Everything the Lord has said, we will do" (Ex 19:8). At His Ascension, Jesus tells His disciples to teach all the nations "to observe all that I have commanded you" (Mt 28:20). At Cana, Mary says: "Do whatever he tells you" (Jn 2:5). Mary invites others to follow Christ in a spousal way—completely and faithfully.

What is it that Jesus tells the servants to do? "Fill the jars" (Jn 2:7). St. Bernard of Clairvaux wrote: "*Habet mundus iste noctes suas et non paucas.*"[13] Contemporary culture is fragmented and unstable. Its Christian roots are eroding as levels of anxiety continue to rise. Spiritual emptiness dominates a once rich

culture. The six empty jars of Cana serve as a useful meta-
phor to describe the culture in which seminarians are formed
and provide an opportunity to think creatively of responses
to the Lord's command to "Fill the jars" in the context of
seminary formation. Each jar represents something lacking
in current society or culture. What are these six jars? They
represent the lack of festivity (joyousness in a feast); the lack
of "gift"; the lack of memory; the lack of prophecy; the lack
of beauty; and the lack of silence.

The First Jar: Lack of Festivity

The first empty jar represents the lack of festivity in
the world. There is a sadness that pervades today's culture,
a mortal sickness in which bitterness dominates people's
private, social, political, and cultural life. Cynicism reigns,
and many are no longer disposed to joy. Advances in science
and technology have not eliminated sadness. A new, "technical" society, rooted in efficiency, has arisen; but it does not
produce real and lasting joy. Why not? Paul VI said that joy
comes from beyond; it is spiritual.[14] While it is convenient to
blame God for many modern ills, it is important to recognize
that these ills result from the *interior* weakness of individuals.
St. John Paul II recognized that at the root of structural or
social sin, there is also personal sin—interior weakness.[15]

Contributing to this sadness is a utilitarian culture that
values people based on what they do, have, and contribute
rather than based on who they are. The push toward an ever-
more technical and efficient society is leading away from the
roots of ancient cultures, which were more concerned about
being and beauty than usefulness and efficiency. The joy of
simply being together and enjoying one another's company is

diminishing. Many have become cynical, convinced that they will live in the condition in which they find themselves, without hope of real improvement. The Church is not unaffected by this condition. The Holy Father himself has mentioned that some Christians celebrate Lent without Easter![16]There is a crisis of joy—even within the Church.

What is the solution? The Eucharist is the Sacrament that nourishes Christian joy. It is the strongest sacramental sign of the Paschal Lordship of Christ, recalling His Victory over sin and death. In the Eucharist, the joy that He has won is preserved and shared. The Eucharist is not incomplete or fading like the pleasures of this world of which we partake to try to experience joy; it is a lasting joy. Joy is fruit of the Holy Spirit, whom Jesus breathed on the Apostles on that first Easter evening![17] The Church celebrates the Eucharist with a spousal joy, the joy of one promised to Christ. The Church brings the world joy when she offers the Eucharist. "Fill the jars." We are to fill the jars with the Eucharistic joy.

Mary teaches Christians that joy is a gift. At the Annunciation, the angel greets her, "Hail, favored one" (Lk 1:28). She, filled to the brim with joy and grace, is the cause of our joy, bringing Jesus to the world, just as she brought joy to Elizabeth and John at the Visitation, modeling true missionary discipleship. As an archetype of the Church, she says, "They have no wine" (Jn 2:3); it is wine that brings joy to the heart of man.[18] She reminds the Church that joy is possible and that believers are to be servants of joy. The joy of being loved by God, especially in the Eucharist, leads the servants to joyfully fill the first jar!

In the context of seminary formation, this joy might be captured by more solemn (yet joy-filled) Eucharistic celebrations. The *horarium* of the day might be adjusted to allow for greater festivity—beginning the day later, having a solemn celebration of lauds or vespers, cancelling other events during solemnities. At the level of human formation, on feasts and solemnities, meals served could be of higher quality, reflecting the joyful occasion. The academic schedule could be modified, shortening periods of study, to create enough time for Adoration or a period of contemplation on a feast. Practically, there are many options open to formators, but feasts and solemnities ought not to be celebrated like ordinary days, which are often dominated by rushing from one class or activity to another. The slower pace and more joy-filled celebration of the seminary day may, in turn, help future priests cultivate a spirituality of joy, joined to the liturgical year, in their parishes.

The Second Jar: The Lack of "Giving"

The Eucharist is a mystery of self-giving. Through His offering on the Cross, Jesus makes a radical gift of Himself to the Father and, in the Eucharist, to us. The miracles of Jesus, whether the multiplication of the loaves or the changing of water into wine, show the super-abundance of the Divine gratuity.

Mary is the Mother of the Son, given to us in the Eucharist. She gives herself to God, especially in her radical "Yes" in response to the call of the Lord at the Annunciation. At Christmastime, the Church celebrates the gift she offered to the world, but her giving continues to Calvary, where what was prophesied in the story of Abraham offering his son Isaac is fulfilled. There, Mary, immersed in sorrow, shares in the Death of her Son. Her presence beneath the Cross, along with the women and John, the Beloved Disciple who is also a priest, unites the Church and all of creation to the offering—to the giving of her Son—to the Father.

Today, despite pockets of generosity, we are scandalized by the ever-increasing selfishness that pervades the world. Statistics tell the story. Eight of the world's wealthiest people have the combined assets of the bottom 50 percent of the world. Half of the world lives on less than $2.50 per day. The poorest 40 percent of the world's population accounts for 5 percent of global income. Twenty-two thousand (22,000) children die each day due to poverty. In 2005, the wealthiest 20 percent of the world consumed 76 percent of the world's resources; whereas the poorest 20 percent consumed only 1.5 percent of the world's resources.[19]

To fill the empty jar, which represents a lack of giving and generosity, the Church needs to challenge the culture of consumption and individualism by ceaselessly pointing to the common good. At Christmas, most people show a special generosity; this is the logic of the gift that Christians must show year-round. The Church is reminded that "a child is born to us; a son is given to us" (Is 9:5). The Infant King calls each person to give—and to make a gift of himself in humble service. This logic of the gift is equally true at Calvary, where the Son handed Himself over for the salvation of the world rather than saving Himself, providing an example of what it means to be both priest and victim. To fill the jars means to cultivate a new spirit of generosity, mindful of the dire poverty in which many are forced to live. Cherishing each person as a response to the gift of the Eucharist is a sure remedy to the selfishness of a throwaway culture.

What are some ways in which this spirit of generosity may be fostered in seminaries? Within the seminary itself, greater solidarity with the poor can be fostered through encouraging simplicity of life with respect to technology, media, decorations, even in diet and accommodation. Although seminarians have limited spending money, they can still be encouraged to be generous, perhaps at such times as World Mission Sunday. A Christmas giving tree could be encouraged during the holiday season to benefit the poor, domestically and globally. Lenten almsgiving can also be intentional to support the most needy. The field of apostolic works lends itself to generosity of time and talent; seminarians should be encouraged to go beyond field education requirements, reflecting on how their presence can be a means of an encounter with Christ, who has generously offered Himself in the Eucharist. Seminary formation seeks to move candidates beyond program requirements to develop the habits and virtues suited for the priestly vocation.

The Third Jar: The Lack of Memory

The third jar represents a lack of memory. Modern man lives in the present moment, risking the loss of his connection with the past and with it, the wisdom of his ancestors. One result of the Enlightenment and modern philosophy is that people have a genuine skepticism in speaking about the future and a distrust of the past. Living in the present, the person moves from one thing to another, presuming that what is most recent is best and that the lessons of the past were useful only for primitive people. At stake is the sense of belonging to a living tradition.

For Christianity, the past is decisive. God acted in history. Salvation began in historical events, and our eschatological future lies in remembering what God has done in the past with hope for the future. Thomas Aquinas captured it well in his *O Sacrum Convivium*: "O Sacred Banquet, in which Christ is received, the memory of his Passion is renewed, the mind is filled with grace, and a pledge of future glory is given to us."[20]

The Eucharist is the sacrament of memory. It is a memorial that recalls the history of grace—what God has done—in Christ, preserving the charity of God and the love that He has for each person. It is a memorial (*anamnesis*). Jesus commands, "Do this in memory of me." Yet, it is not a simple remembrance or repetition but the celebration and remembrance of a mystery that makes present the saving Sacrifice of Calvary in an unbloody manner.

Mary is the woman of the memory. In her are joined the graces and hopes of the people of Israel. Through her Son, all that was prophesied is fulfilled. She is rooted in the history and faith of her people. She believes as one who belongs to a people whom God has chosen as His own. Her *Magnificat* captures the fact that her faith is directed toward the God of her Fathers. In her *Magnificat*, she holds the memory of the great works of God in the past and foresees the future works of Divine Mercy for future generations.

Mary is the living memory of the Church. She teaches the Church about the duty to tell others about the love God has for them. The Church has a role in communicating the story of salvation history, while giving prophetic witness, thanksgiving, and praise to the God who saves. Her response will motivate others to give witness and to encourage trust and hope in God. To fill the jar means learning from Mary how to cultivate the memory of the things of God, recalling His covenants, especially the new and eternal covenant made in the Blood of Jesus. By telling the story of salvation history, the Church provides society and culture with a way of recovering its lost unity. Today, there is a danger of living in the present moment in an ephemeral way—without looking to the future: to our destiny and the end times.

In seminary, spiritual and liturgical formation, Marian devotion—pausing for the Angelus or communal recitation of the Rosary, recalling the mysteries of Christ and the presence of Mary—can foster a spirit of remembrance and contemplation. Concluding the day with Night Prayer and a Marian hymn, followed by silence, is another way of asking for her maternal intercession as one continues to remember the moments of fragility and grace that have occurred throughout the day.

The Fourth Empty Jar: The Lack of Prophecy

The fourth jar represents prophecy. Paul VI said, "The Church needs a perennial Pentecost. She needs fire in her heart, words on her lips, prophecy in her outlook."[21] Today, there is a loss of the sense of our final destiny. Without desiring to live in the Spirit, people still want to know the future. While science and reason can tell many things, they cannot accurately predict all future events. People are losing sight of an *ultimate* future. They look at larger cultural, political, and social trends and notice changes. Where is society headed? When people respond, "We are headed toward the future," one wonders what they mean.

The Eucharist is the sacrament of a future with God. The Church not only speaks of an ultimate future but also carries out works capable of bringing man to the beatific vision and his eschatological end. She baptizes, creating the condition for adoption as children of God and heirs to the Kingdom. She celebrates the Eucharist, the pledge of future glory. She witnesses to charity as a response to the Sacrament of Charity, in anticipation of the Final Judgment, in which the treatment of the least of our brothers and sisters is decisive. The Eucharist inaugurates the new times and makes the life of the People of God a dynamic journey toward the presence of the Living God. Its celebration, especially on Sunday, is a reminder that work is relative; people ought to rest on that day and to rejoice in the Lord.

Mary lives her prophetic charism in view of her destiny. The mystery of the Assumption captures this truth. She was assumed body and soul into heaven and now shares in the glory of heaven. She is the image of the Church in her perfection—what the Church is called to be. She is a reminder of future glory, offering prophetic witness that the promises of the Lord will be fulfilled.

Consumed by his daily tasks, modern man makes decisions, given his brief time upon this earth, without remembering his past or looking forward to his destiny. Existing in a climate of nihilism, which has left many with a feeling of despair and emptiness, the person discovers that a desire for the Absolute remains, for the world has been unable to provide satisfactory answers to the deepest questions of life. Even if the landscape appears as a moral and spiritual desert, created by nihilistic philosophies and ideologies, the Catholic recalls that God still searches for His flock—even in the desert—and leads it to the Promised Land. Filling the jar means recovering a sense of mission—proposing and re-proposing the wealth of the Church's spiritual tradition. To fill the jar means witnessing to eternal truths to the end; the lives of the modern martyrs give prophetic witness to things eternal.

In seminary formation, formators might concern themselves with helping seminarians to use Sunday as a day of prayer, rest, and fraternity rather than as a day to be filled with constant activity, especially academic work that has been left undone to Sunday. To realize this goal, greater effort should be made to help seminarians manage time during the week, not waste it in idleness or juvenile activities. Building a seminary culture in which virtual fasting is commonplace creates a climate for contemplation to flourish and for reflection, in openness to the Spirit, on how the prophetic charism is actuated in one's life. Increasing the opportunities for Eucharistic Adoration may provide seminarians with the opportunity simply to *be* and to contemplate things eternal.

With that in mind, a word may be said about prophecy and life in the Spirit. In seminary formation, greater emphasis could be placed on the role of spiritual charisms and gifts. While some seminarians are familiar with the charismatic movement, others are not or show little interest, dismissing the movement in an ideological way. The same could be said of lay ecclesial movements within the Church. How is the Spirit of God at work within these movements that represent a prophetic voice in the Church today? Seminary formation ought to familiarize seminarians with these movements, as well as with the prophetic charisms of religious communities, so that the ordained might see them not as competitors or mere resources but, rather, might allow their particular charisms to contribute to the growth of the local Church and parish.

The Fifth Jar: The Lack of Beauty

At the end of Vatican II, the Council Fathers sent a message to artists, writing: "The world in which we live needs beauty in order not to sink into despair. Beauty, like truth, brings joy to the human heart and is that precious fruit which resists the erosion of time, which unites generations and enables them to be one in admiration!"[22]

Beauty is a fundamental category of being, nature, man, and God. Is ours a world of beauty? The amount of brutality seen on the news answers the question. Many live in a world characterized by brokenness, disproportion, and a loss of sense of distance and propriety. In a world marked by brokenness, people recognize when something, which was once whole, is now shattered. Society is characterized by fractures: between past, present, and future; between doing and being; between private and public ethics; between ethical demands and truth; between life and love, and so on. These things, little by little, have been separated, leading to a world of moral and ethical relativism.

The ugliness of the modern world is seen in the lack of proper proportion. There is a genuine loss of a sense of measure and pace. Life is marked by excess, by living without breaks or contemplation. People are increasingly immoderate in speech, dress, consumption of food and alcohol, and sizes of homes and cars. There is little room left for stillness, proportion, nuance, and asceticism. In the end, much of what remains is gross and grotesque.

Beauty is undermined by a loss of a sense of distance and propriety. Modern society is characterized by a lack of sobriety, vulgarity, and coarseness in speech. There is an unhealthy familiarity between people that, at times, does not respect roles and authority in life, leading to disharmony in society and family life. Cardinal Sarah notes:

> Silence teaches us a great rule of the spiritual life: familiarity does not promote intimacy; on the contrary, a proper distance is a condition for communion. Humanity advances toward love through adoration. Sacred silence, laden with the adored presence, opens the way to mystical silence, full of loving intimacy.[23]

In contrast, there is the Eucharist, the icon of beauty. It is called the beautiful feast and the beautiful "Bread." There is a beauty at the Mass in the family of God, gathered together with a father (in the person of the bishop or priest) and a mother (with the Blessed Virgin present). There is active listening and fruitful discussion, exteriorly and interiorly. The whole family is strengthened and nourished. The image of the Church at prayer, nourished by Word and Sacrament, joined to the Church in heaven, is beautiful.

The Marian presence reminds us of beauty. She, who is called *tota pulchra*, is beautifully depicted in art, but what is truly beautiful about her is the grace of God at work in her. She was conceived immaculately and lived in full conformity with Christ. Believers are attracted to her interior beauty. As the fairest daughter of our race, she possesses a holiness that exemplifies true beauty for disciples and draws them close.

To fill the jar with beauty means to commit to holiness of life. In seminary formation, this takes the form not only of fulfillment of formational benchmarks in the spiritual dimension, but it can also take the form of greater accountability to one's peers and to one's spiritual director. This is particularly true with respect to addictive behaviors (i.e., pornography, alcohol, and so on). Commitment to holiness demands transparency and accountability. Providing more opportunities for spiritual direction and sacramental reconciliation will enhance this commitment.

Mary, in her humble acceptance of God's will in her life, shows us the way of beauty, the *via pulchritudinis*. She demonstrates that seeking God's will leads us to that which is true, good, and beautiful. Commitment to the Truth—to the person of Jesus Christ and that which is revealed by the Church—in the classroom and beyond, will help restore beauty. Seminarians might reflect on their treatment of creation and their neighbor, which show forth the beauty of God. Dostoevsky said, "Beauty will save the world,"[24] but it is really the beauty of Christ—the beautiful Shepherd—that attracts and saves the world.

The Sixth Empty Jar: The Lack of Silence

Silence belongs to the original experience of man. Adam was created in solitude. Silence is necessary to reflect and to search for answers and meaning. The current culture of noise and its lack of silence threatens our civilization. A new Babel, a society in which people talk past one another, unable to listen, to communicate effectively, to understand, or to think deeply, is emerging. The "heart" does not have the silence it needs to listen to others or even to listen to itself. Developments in technology have made silence rare. Without silence, it becomes increasingly difficult to develop one's spiritual life, especially when God speaks in a whisper.

Cardinal Sarah cautions:

There is a real warning that our civilization needs to hear. If our intellects can no longer close their eyes, if we no longer know how to be quiet, then we will be deprived of mystery, of its light, which is beyond darkness, of its beauty, which is beyond all beauty. Without mystery, we are reduced to the banality of earthly things.[25]

In contrast, there is the silence of the three days in the tomb as the Breviary recounts:

Something strange is happening. There is a great silence on earth today, a great silence and stillness. The whole earth keeps silence because the King is asleep. The earth trembled and is still because God has fallen asleep in the flesh and he has raised up all who have slept ever since the world began. God has died in the flesh and hell trembles.[26]

The Eucharist is the sacrament of silence. Jesus, present in the Eucharist, dwells in the tabernacle in silence and speaks silently to the human heart. How many come to churches to find comfort in His presence, to pour out their hearts, and to adore Him in silence!

Mary is a woman of silence. At the Annunciation, she was silently recollected when the angel appeared to her. One can imagine the silence of that holy night on which Mary gave birth to the Child in Bethlehem. Later, in the Temple, she contemplated all the events and the words of holy Simeon in her heart. She keeps great silence over the early years of Jesus' life. Even in His public life, in John's Gospel, between Cana and Calvary, Mary is silent. At the foot of the Cross, Mary silently receives the words of Jesus. She is silent in prayer with the Apostles at Pentecost when she again encounters the Spirit who overshadows her. She is a woman of silence.

But Mary speaks at Cana: "Do whatever he tells you" (Jn 2:5). He says, "Fill the jars" (Jn 2:7). To fill this jar means intentionally to build a culture of silence—that is, to have a little more silence daily for prayer. It means having silence in the Liturgy—after the readings and homily or after Communion—and arriving early to prepare and staying afterward to give thanks. The culture of silence demands guarding our speech—from profanity, hurtful words, gossip, and idle chatter. The culture of silence allows individuals and whole communities to be more open to the promptings of the Holy Spirit, who prays for us even when we do not know how to pray as we ought.[27] It is the Spirit, who hovered over the waters at the dawn of creation, who will renew the face of the earth. It is the Spirit of the new Pentecost who conquers the disunity of the new Babel.

Conclusion

The six empty jars—festivity, self-giving, memory, prophecy, beauty, and silence—must be filled in response to the gift of the Eucharist, central to the life of the priest. Cana is an invitation to heed the words of Mary, "Do whatever he tells you"; and of Jesus, "Fill the jars." Through obedience to these words, the glory of the Lord will be manifest. These two commands provide a pattern for the life of the disciple and priest.

At Cana, Mary instructs believers to listen to the voice of her Son. In silence, she mastered the art of listening to the voice of God and invites us to do the same. If we do not listen, we cannot respond as she did at the Annunciation—with a definitive "Yes." This spirit of listening to the voice of God matured so that she could experience the saving event of the Sacrifice of Calvary in a profound way. There, she heard: "Woman, behold, your son . . . Behold, your mother" (Jn 19:26-27). There, too, she heard: "It is finished" (Jn 19:30). In all this, she provides an example of stopping to hear the voice of God and contemplating it.

The time spent in seminary is a privileged time for listening. Returning to Cana, seminary formators and seminarians listen to Mary, who says, "Do whatever He tells you" and to Jesus, who says, "Fill the Jars." Mary and Jesus help the Church discover the balance between contemplation and action. Christ asks the servants—and, with them, all disciples—to fill the jars. This requires openness to his miraculous power and strong faith. It demands humility, recognizing that the Divine is necessary to perform the miracle. Still, each person can do his part to fill the jars. In exercising the virtues of faith and humility, one recognizes the Lordship of Jesus and one's baptismal responsibility.

By bringing a little water to our world to fill these empty jars, disciples acknowledge that Christ can do a lot with our offerings. At Cana, He transforms water into wine, inaugurating the messianic times with a new wine for a new era. The new wine is the nuptial gift of the Messiah to His Bride. The water of the Old Covenant filled the jars to the brim; but at Cana, Christ transformed it. His Word, His power transforms and transfigures. Through His miracle, He transforms a tragic situation into a joyful celebration! Through His miracle, He shows His glory!

The Lord never ceases to work new miracles. Eucharistic worship also transforms every aspect of our lives. St. Paul says, "Whether you eat or drink, or whatever you do, do everything for the glory of God" (1 Cor 10:31). Priests, seminarians, and formators in their actions—in their filling of the jars daily—are called to offer true worship to God. There is a Eucharistic nature to Christian life. Each day, in response to the call, the disciple (the seminarian) is progressively transfigured to reflect the image of the Son of God—to show His glory and to draw others to believe in Him.

NOTES

1. V Conferencia General del Episcopado Latinoamericano y del Caribe, *Documento conclusivo*, CELAM, Aparecida 2007, 37.

2. Congregation for Clergy, *Ratio Fundamentalis Institutionis Sacerdotalis* The Gift of the Priestly Vocation, in Supplement to *L'Osservatore Romano*, 8 December 2016, sec. 59-60.

3. Ibid., sec. 84c.

4. Ibid., sec. 29.

5. Ibid., sec. 41.

6. See John 2:1-12.

7. Michele G. Masciarelli, *La maestra. Lezioni mariane a Cana* (Libreria Editrice Vaticana: Città del Vaticano, 2002), 122; "Maria e l'Eucaristia dinanzi alle carenze umane," in *Maria e l'Eucaristia* (Centro di Cultura Mariana: Roma, 2000), 63-144.

8. See John 2:11-12.

9. *Ratio Fundamentalis*, Introduction, sec. 8.

10. *Catechism of the Catholic Church*, 2nd ed. (Libreria Editrice Vaticana: Città del Vaticano, 1997), sec. 2618.

11. Ibid., sec. 1335.

12. See Exodus 19.

13. Bernard of Clairvaux, *Serm. In Cantica Canticorum*, *LXXV*, 10.

14. Paul VI, *Gaudete in Domino* (1975), *Acta Apostolicae Sedis* (*AAS*) 67 (1975): 289-322, at 291.

15. John Paul II, *Reconciliatio et Paenitentiae* (1984), *AAS* 77 (1985): 185-275, 18.

16. Francis, *Evangelii Gaudium* (2013), *AAS* 105 (2013): 1019-1137, sec. 6. Pope Francis also laments the sterile pessimism and defeatism of many Christians, calling them (at sec. 85) "sourpusses."

17. See John 20:19:31.

18. See Psalms 104:15.

19. Oxfam International, "An economy for the 99%," 16 January 2017 at: www.oxfam.org/sites/www.oxfam.org/files/file_attachments/bp-economy-for-99-percent-160117-en.pdf, (accessed on July 20, 2017).

20. "O Sacrum Convivium," (United States Conference of Catholic Bishops version).

21. Paul VI, General Audience, 29 November 1972. Available at: http://w2.vatican.va/content/paul-vi/it/audiences/1972/documents/hf_p-vi_and_19721129.html, (accessed July 21, 2017).

22. Paul VI, "Message to Artists at the Solemn Conclusion of the Second Vatican Ecumenical Council," 8 December 1965: *AAS* 58 (1966), 12-13.

23.   Robert Sarah, *The Power of Silence: Against the Dictatorship of Noise* (Ignatius Press: San Francisco, 2017), 122.

24.   Fyodor Dostoyevsky, *The Idiot.*

25.   Ibid., 125.

26.   Liturgy of the Hours, Office of Readings, Holy Saturday. The author of the text is unknown, but the text was likely written in Greek and dates to the fourth century and can be found in *Patrologia Graeca* 43, 439, 462ff.

27.   See Romans 8:26.

CPSIA information can be obtained
at www.ICGtesting.com
Printed in the USA
FSHW020343141118
53652FS

9 780998 116457